PARENTING YOUR TEENAGER IN THE 1990's

Practical Information & Advice
About Adolescent Development
& Contemporary Issues

DAVID ELKIND, PH.D.

Modern Learning Press

Rosemont, New Jersey 08556

Cataloging in Publication Data

Elkind, David, 1931-
 Parenting your teenager in the 1990's : practical information & advice about adolescent development & contemporary issues / David Elkind.
 p. cm.
 Includes bibliographical references and index.
 ISBN 1-56762-015-9

 1. Parent and teenager. 2. Adolescent psychology.
I. Title. II. Title: Parenting your teenager in the nineteen-
nineties.

 HQ799.15.E55 1993   649'.125
                                    QBI93-1263

ACKNOWLEDGEMENTS

A book may have one author, but many editors. This is particularly true of the present volume, which grew out of a collection of columns originally published in Parents Magazine.

I would first like to acknowledge and thank the several editors who worked with me on the columns over the years: Cynthia Carney Johnson, Marilyn Mayo, Roy DeLaMar, Patty McCormick, Wendy Schuman, and Pam Abrams. I also want to express my deep appreciation to Elizabeth Crow, who first asked me to write for Parents Magazine, and to Annie Murphy, who replaced Elizabeth as the editor-in-chief of the magazine. Both were always supportive of the columns and have made my association with Parents Magazine a most warm and memorable one.

I also want to thank the staff members of Modern Learning Press who have worked on this book. In particular, I would like to thank Robert Low, whose thoughtful and sensitive editing of the manuscript has made it a much better book.

And, finally, I would like to express my gratitude to the many teenagers and parents with whom I have worked over the years. They taught me much of what I have passed on in this book.

CONTENTS

PREFACE

In 1987, I began writing a monthly column on adolescence for Parents Magazine. During that year and the years that followed, the editors and I would discuss potential topics for the columns, trying to touch on a variety of issues that ranged in tone from the upbeat and light-hearted to the more serious and complicated. In addition, we made an effort to combine topics that were timely — such as concern about the environment — with topics that were timeless — such as adolescent passions.

The columns were well-received, and in 1992 I had an opportunity to review all that I had written during the previous five years. In doing so, it seemed to me that if these individual essays were of help to parents, the complete collection in a single volume might also be useful. The publisher and editor of Modern Learning Press agreed, suggesting that I add an introduction to the book and an overview of each chapter, in addition to revising the columns to make them as current and cohesive as possible. So, here we are.

When I originally wrote and later revised the columns, I drew upon my many years of experience working with young people as a clinical psychologist. Early in my career, I had worked at a residential treatment center for young people, and I later served as a staff psychologist on the adolescent ward at a psychiatric hospital. I gained additional experience working as a consultant with numerous outpatient clinics, and as a consulting juvenile court psychologist both in Denver, Colorado and Rochester, New York.

DAVID ELKIND

In addition to my clinical work with young people, I called upon the information I had compiled while conducting a number of research studies involving adolescents. These studies dealt with topics such as concept formation, problem solving, self-consciousness, and religious experience. Also included in the mix was my experience working with individual adolescents in my private practice, and my stint as an Explorer Scout leader for disadvantaged youth. Last, but surely not least, I included some memories of my own adolescence, as well as some of my experiences as the father of three sons.

In these columns, I have tried first of all to provide parents with solid, research-based information about adolescent growth and development. Secondly, I have tried to explain some of the major problems facing parents and teenagers today. And, finally, I have attempted to offer advice and suggestions for dealing with different issues that most parents of adolescents encounter at one time or other.

Throughout the columns, I have tried to convey my appreciation of the fact that both teenagers and their parents are unique individuals, and that there are no "one size fits all" prescriptions. What works for one parent may not work for another, and that says only that we are different, not that we are better or worse than one another.

What I believe is most important, and what I have tried to emphasize throughout this book, is the need for parents to appreciate their teenager's perspective. If we make the effort to see the world through an adolescent's eyes, we can obtain a fresh understanding of his or her behavior, as well as how we might best respond to it.

At the same time, our perspective as parents is important, too, and we need to help teenagers see the world from our standpoint. It is this ongoing effort — to understand and communicate with one another in whatever style suits us — which offers the best hope for dealing successfully with the pains and pleasures of rearing an adolescent.

INTRODUCTION

The teenage years — the period during which young people make the transition from childhood to adulthood — are often stressful both for teenagers and for us as parents. In part, these stresses arise from the suddenness of the adolescent transition, in part from the difficulties of our own mid-life transitions, and in part from the social context in which all these transitions occur.

Nature has a wonderfully ironic sense of humor. She gives us 10-year-olds who have it all together as children. They like themselves, their siblings, their teachers, and their parents. While they are interested in growing up, they truly enjoy being children, as well as being with and doing things with their families. We, their parents, are respected, admired, attended to and, for the most part, heeded. Nature thus lulls us into dismissing as overblown the horror stories we have heard of adolescent storms and stress, leaving us hopeful that the teen years may not be so bad after all.

Young people, however, continue to grow. They turn 11 and then 12. Whereas before, we parents could do no wrong, now suddenly we can do no right. The warm, outgoing 10-year-old has become a caustically critical 12-year-old, and we will not see the likes of the 10-year-old again until our teenager turns 16. In the meantime, we have to deal with the teenage struggles to adjust to a new body, new feelings, new interests and longings, and new reasoning abilities.

Not surprisingly, the young adolescent sometimes shows wide mood swings, switching between elation and depression, or becoming overly self-confident and then overly self-critical. While the teenager demands to be treated as an adult, he or she can quickly revert to childish language and behavior. The well-balanced 10-year-old simply has not prepared us for the chaos of the early adolescent years.

For us parents, the churlishness of the teenager may come at a particularly bad time. When our children turn adolescent, many of us are in our late thirties, or in our forties or early fifties. This is a period when we begin to worry about aging and related physical changes such as hair loss and weight gain. We may also be forced to reassess our career goals and aspirations. Instead of measuring ourselves against those whose level of success we will never reach, we may now compare ourselves with those of our peers whom we have left behind. We no longer consider our lives from the perspective of an unlimited future, but rather from the perspective of how many years we have left.

Our teenagers can make this process of adjusting to the realities of mid-life more difficult. Their youthful vigor — both physical and intellectual — intensifies our own sense of declining powers. Their optimism about the future and what they are going to achieve may make more acute our own sense of not having attained all that we wished. It is almost as if adolescents were maliciously visited upon us to make our mid-life passage all the more troublesome and painful. And, because of our own efforts to cope with an important transition, we may lose patience with our teenagers, who are trying to manage their own equally troubling and stressful transition to adulthood.

As if these biological and psychological considerations were not enough to make adolescence difficult for both us and our offspring, contemporary society has made it even more treacherous. Up until mid-century, society regarded teenagers as *immature* — as in need of adult guidance, standards, and limits to successfully reach adulthood themselves. The major social institutions that impact upon the family — the schools, the media, the legal profession — accepted and reinforced the image of adolescent immaturity. Schools, for example, offered many faculty-organized clubs (debating, drama, cooking, and gardening) which provided adult mentors who taught young people valuable skills. The media depicted teenagers as getting into scrapes from which they had to be rescued by adults. And, the legal system attempted to protect young people through the passage of child labor laws and compulsory schooling legislation.

Within the confines of perceived immaturity and its social reinforcement, adolescents felt secure and protected. They were comfortable challenging parents' and teachers' authority, because they knew adults accepted these confrontations for what they were — namely, efforts at adolescent self-definition. Parents, in turn, though dealing with their own mid-life issues, still regarded themselves as mature adults who were more knowledgeable and wiser than their offspring. This made it easier for parents to accept teenagers' youth and vigor as a characteristic of a stage of life, and not as a vindictive celebration of their own decline. Since mid-century, however, we have changed our perception of adolescents. Now, at the end of the century, we no longer perceive them as immature, but rather as *sophisticated* —

ready and able to deal with all of life's vicissitudes. This perception of adolescent sophistication has been accepted by the schools, by the media, and by the legal profession, all of which now reflect and reinforce it. For example, many contemporary schools no longer provide clubs for youth, but they do offer sex education and drug education programs. This reflects educators' recognition of the fact that sexual activity and drug use are now viable options for teenagers. Likewise, the media now portray adolescents as sophisticated, rather than as naive and immature. There are teenage vamps on the afternoon "soaps," and adolescents are also depicted as being sexually active in both films and prime-time television series. The legal system, in turn, is now geared to protecting young people's rights, rather than protecting young people themselves. A lowering of the age for statutory rape in some states is but one illustration of this new emphasis.

The change in our perception of teenagers, it must be admitted, is also in keeping with our more varied lifestyles as parents. Dual-income, single-parent, and re-married families are now more numerous than the traditional nuclear family, in which the biological mother stays home to rear the children while the biological father provides all the financial support. Our new parental lifestyles, together with the changes in the economy, often afford us less time and energy to devote to our teenage offspring than was true in the past.

These new lifestyles and pressures can make us more willing to accept the perception of adolescent sophistication. When viewed as sophisticated, teenagers demand much less from us in the way of support and of setting rules and limits. In a very real sense, the perception of adolescents as sophisticated gives us a rationale — as parents and as a society — for abrogating our adult responsibilities to young people. Even those of us parents who are responsible, and who do set rules and limits, often receive little or no support from other parents, the schools, the media, and society in general.

One result of all these changes, therefore, is that end-of-the-century teenagers are left to their own devices much more often than adolescents of earlier generations. Yet, teenagers are still the young of the species, and like the young of all species, they require adult guidance, limits, and standards. Without these, teenagers lack a system of morals and values on which to hone their own set of standards. Not having such a system to define themselves against is stressful, and makes young people vulnerable to many of society's unhealthy avenues of stress reduction.

These trends are taking their toll on the teenagers of the 1990's. Before mid-century, most adolescent deaths were due to diseases such as polio and tuberculosis. Thankfully, medical science has now conquered these mortal dangers to youth. Today, however, we lose proportionately the same or even more young people to stress-related behaviors. This has been called the *new morbidity*. For example, some ten thousand teenagers die each year in automobile accidents, and another forty thousand young people are injured or maimed. Most of these accidents occur on the weekends, when young people have been drinking. We have more than 2 million adolescent alcoholics, and the suicide rate for teenagers has tripled since mid-century. In addition, the homicide rate for teenagers between 14 and 19-years-old is the second highest of any age group. Venereal disease among teenagers is epidemic, and though the incidence of AIDS is relatively low among adolescents, they are a group that is at risk because a significant number do not use any form of protection.

The new societal perception of adolescent sophistication, along with the stress it induces, are the major factors responsible for the new morbidity. The trends are linked in that teenagers react to stress in the same way that adults do; they try to escape it by engaging in risky behaviors.

To address the new morbidity, we have to challenge the perception of adolescent sophistication. Fortunately, perceptions can be changed. We have seen how the perception of smoking has been transformed over the last quarter century. From a habit that was once regarded as a symbol of refinement and sophistication, it has become a symbol of self-indulgence and self-destruction. If we are going to reverse the trends that result in the new morbidity, we need to alter our perception of young people.

While end-of-the-century adolescents do show signs of sophistication, we need to see them as *growing* in sophistication, but not quite there yet. Once we come to perceive teenagers in this way, we begin to reassert our adulthood, and provide young people with the value systems they need to make their own successful transitions to adulthood.

Accordingly, in this book I have tried to accomplish several different goals. First of all, wherever possible, I have tried to provide a portrait of normal adolescent development, as a general guide to understanding and dealing with young people. If we know that certain behaviors are typical of a particular age group, rather than unique creations of our teenager designed to drive us mad, we can handle them in a more appropriate fashion.

Secondly, I have tried to be sensitive to your needs, feelings, and aspirations as a parent. We all need to remember that parents are people too, and our feelings of hurt, frustration, and anger are often quite healthy and legitimate. I have tried to suggest ways of expressing these feelings without doing injury to your teenager's sense of self.

Finally, throughout this book, I have addressed issues of contemporary society and the many pressures placed upon today's teenagers. It is very tempting and understandable for parents to feel helpless in regard to the incessant bombardment of sex, violence, and materialism directed at adolescents. However, we can exert more influence as parents than we sometimes give ourselves credit for. There are actions we can take to counter some of the societal pressures and temptations, and I have suggested a few strategies of this sort. Even though we cannot do as much as we would like, we must do as much as we can.

The 1990's are a difficult time to be a teenager's parent, but the difficulties are not insurmountable. If we try to respect our adolescent's uniqueness — his or her own special talents and abilities — we are on the right track. If we set limits with firmness and love, and don't worry about our teenager's not always liking us, we are moving along at a healthy pace. And, if we can, at the same time, fully support the young person's own lifestyle choices, we are reaching our destination as parents.

To be sure, these goals are sometimes contradictory, and setting limits may sometimes conflict with supporting a teenager's lifestyle choices. Perhaps our hardest job as parents is to make our best judgement as to when to set limits and when to encourage teenagers to follow the path they have chosen. We will, at times, make mistakes, for we are only human after all. But, if we make the effort to be the sort of adults we would like our adolescents to become, we can at least proceed with the confidence that we are meeting our responsibilities as parents, and doing the best we can for our teenage offspring.

1
EMOTIONAL AND PSYCHOLOGICAL DEVELOPMENT

OVERVIEW

At around the age of puberty, young people attain a new set of mental abilities that vastly extend the range of their feelings, emotions, and thoughts. These new abilities enable adolescents to deal with possibilities, to conceive of ideals and conditions far different than the reality they encounter, and to think about thinking. It is these new mental abilities that account for the changes we parents observe in our teenagers' passions, concerns, and fears, as well as in their new-found capacity to cope with anxiety and stress.

In many ways, teenagers are becoming more adult than childlike in their feelings and emotions, which are much more complex and multi-layered than they were during childhood. Whereas children simply like something or dislike it, teenagers like something under some circumstances but may dislike it under others. It is this multi-layered quality of teenager's feelings and emotions that accounts for some of the behaviors — such as eating disorders and depression — which appear for the first time at this age level.

It is also in adolescence, for example, that young people come to identify with a group, expressing themselves as part of the group in ways they never dare to do on their own. Adolescence, too, is the period during which young people begin to "worry" about the possible, whereas children are more likely to have "fears" about the here and now.

On the other hand, some of the behaviors we see in adolescents — such as shyness — are carried over from childhood but can become amplified. Thanks to their new mental abilities and their capacity to think about other people's thinking, teenagers now experience a new self-consciousness, which in some is manifested as extreme shyness. Teenagers also begin to see media idols as setting standards of physical attractiveness against which the teens compare their own physical characteristics. Not surprisingly, when some teens believe they are too far from the standard, they may engage in extreme behaviors and develop dangerous syndromes such as anorexia or bulimia.

Adolescents also begin to demonstrate adult character traits such as courage and zest for life in an almost pure, undiluted form. Many teenagers are so full of energy that they take on a multitude of activities, over and beyond what might be expected. While some teens thrive on this activity overload, others have to be encouraged to cut back. And, sometimes even fully involved adolescents can have periods of low mood and depression. At such times, young people greatly benefit from parental support.

One type of support we can provide is to reinforce our teenager's sense of self-worth, particularly when the young person encounters experiences that might diminish it. Adolescents growing up in today's world encounter stresses that were unknown to previous generations, and while we cannot change the world that is producing these stressors, we can help to counter them by talking often and openly with teens about issues that are — or that might be — troubling them.

There are several goals we should try to help our teenagers attain as part of their emotional and psychological development. Certainly, one of the most important — and most stressful for adolescents and parents — is "graduating" from childhood. Adolescents are, in part, reluctant to give up some of the prerogatives of childhood, and parents are sometimes reluctant to give up the prerogatives of parenthood. We help young people most by accepting their growth and supporting their progress towards maturity.

Another important goal is to help our teenagers attain a healthy sense of self-esteem. Self-esteem is not necessarily — and probably should not be — an unbridled sense of one's own personal worth. A healthy sense of self-esteem always includes an appreciation of one's weaknesses and sore points. A third goal is to help teenagers learn to cope with stress in healthy ways, rather than ways that are self-destructive. If young people leave adolescence with a healthy sense of self and effective coping skills, they are well on their way to a successful transition into adulthood.

APPRECIATING YOUR
TEEN'S PASSIONS

As a teenager, I recall watching throngs of screaming young women waiting outside a theater to see Frank Sinatra perform. I thought, rather enviously, that there was something unique about "Frankie" that made so many young women swoon. But, over the years, I have observed successive generations respond in the same way to Elvis, the Beatles, Michael Jackson, Madonna, and Prince. This exuberance of emotion in response to a performer is but one expression of adolescent passions.

Adolescent passions are often displayed *en masse* — at sports events or rock concerts where there are many other people who feel the same way. Thanks to the intellectual abilities that appear at around the age of 11 or 12, adolescents can construct much broader and more abstract categories than they could when they were younger. One resulting realization for a teenager is that he or she is a member of an international age group — a teenager among teenagers.

This new sense of group identity and belonging contributes to the public expression of adolescents' passions. As a member of a group, teenagers feel comfortable giving voice to feelings they might be embarrassed to display on their own. In fact, their identification with a group allows teenagers to express many new and powerful emotions for which there are few, if any, individual outlets. That is why participation in mass events of a psychological nature can be therapeutic for teenagers, as well as for adults.

Of course, not all adolescent passions are linked to mass events. Some teenagers become passionate very early about what will eventually be their life's work, whether in literature, science, music, or sports.

Other adolescent passions are inter-personal. The adolescent crush reflects the teenager's newfound ability to construct ideals, as well as his or her readiness to form new emotional attachments. To a teenager, the young man or woman who is the object of affection appears perfect. The teenager will not hear anything negative about the person, and friendships with same-sex peers may also be defended just as passionately.

What Parents Can Do

It is easy for us adults to forget the depth and fervor of adolescent passions. The emotions a teenager feels are far from being novel on the human stage, but they are new to the teenager. If we appreciate this fact, it may be easier to be sympathetic toward an adolescent who seems too involved or intense in regard to a particular activity or person.

As parents, it helps if we can acknowledge how important these passions are to our teenager, and if we demonstrate that we can accept and sometimes even admire these enthusiasms. Once we communicate this acceptance, adolescents will be more willing to listen if we suggest that they need to spend more time on other activities or broaden their circle of friends. However, we also have to make it clear to them that we cannot accept unhealthy passions, such as those for drugs or gambling. Professional help is often needed to help teenagers master these sorts of passions.

WHAT'S GREAT ABOUT TEENAGERS

"Why do you think we are so terrible?" a teenage girl asked me at a recent forum for teenagers and their parents. Then, she continued, "You always blame us for everything. A few kids do something wrong at the skating rink or at the mall, and pretty soon you close the rink or don't let us in the mall after seven!"

I had to admit that adults do sometimes behave as if *all* teenagers were a menace. I also reminded her that teenagers sometimes behave as if *all* adults were monsters.

Both positions are extremes. Generalizations about a particular age group, like generalizations about religious or ethnic groups, overlook the wide range of individual differences within any given group. So, rather than discuss teenagers in general, I want to reminisce about some of the individual teenagers I knew when I was an adolescent. As adults, recalling those teenagers we admired can help us appreciate the admirable qualities of today's teenagers.

Courage in the Face of Fear

Russell and I became friends in junior high school in Detroit during the 1940's. We both enjoyed books and often rode to the public library together on our bikes. Then, the race riots began. Russell was one of the few blacks in our school, and I was sure Russell would stay home. But, he came to school every day. He never talked about the fear he must have experienced in walking past the National Guardsmen. Nor did he complain about those students who made insulting statements behind his back — or to his face. "Consider the source," he told me.

Soon after the riots ended, my family moved, and I lost touch with Russell. But, I have often thought of him since then. I remembered him during the battles of the civil rights movement in the 1960's. And, I think of him again today when I read of the racial bigotry in some of our schools and colleges. His willingness to challenge hatred, rather than respond in kind, is a testament to the courage of all young people who will not be humbled by prejudice and discrimination.

An Enthusiasm for Life

Although most of my high school friends were boys, I did have one female friend. Sandy was not really pretty; her nose was too long, and her figure had to be described as flat rather than curvy. But, she had a great personality, and being with her was always fun. Sandy never failed to have a project going: putting on a play, selling raffle tickets for charity, and falling in love all became wonderful adventures. Her enthusiasms were infectious, and she often coaxed me out of my shell to aid her in one of her new projects. To me, Sandy was what being young was all about.

Doing It His Way

Harold and I were never close friends. I remember him as something of a loner. We did have a math class together, which gave me a chance to know him a little better. When the teacher returned our final exams to us, Harold was angry and rebellious. Although he had reached the right answers, he did not use the procedures the teacher had told us to use. He came up with his own way of solving the problems and thought those that the teacher showed us were rather tedious and unimaginative. I suggested that he talk to the teacher, but he told me, "You do it their way, or else." Harold dropped out of school after the eleventh grade.

Some years later, I was reminiscing with a high school friend I had been out of touch with for some time. "Do you remember Harold?" he asked. "I met him on a plane a couple of years ago. He's with a major computer company now, travelling all over the world servicing mainframes, and he's a real hot shot. They even sent him to college. He's making a bundle." Good for you, Harold, was my reaction.

What Parents Can Do

Like these young people I admired, today's teenagers have qualities that make them special. Before we parents generalize about teens, we need to acknowledge that they have as much to offer as the teens we once knew. Today, just as yesterday, teenagers are courageous, full of life, rebellious, and much, much more. These traits are what made them so great when I was young, and what continues to make them wonderful today.

WHAT MAKES TEENAGERS ANXIOUS

In the mid-1980's, the media reported survey data suggesting that nuclear war was a major concern among teenagers. While those surveys raised the issue of nuclear war, however, they did not evaluate young people's anxiety about nuclear war in comparison with other issues. When we look at studies in which young people are asked to list their own concerns, nuclear war is seldom, if ever, mentioned. This is even more true today, now that the cold war is at an end and the nuclear threat has greatly diminished.

Today, as in the past, adolescents are most concerned about issues that affect them directly, rather than more abstract, societal dangers. This is shown by the periodic Gallup Youth surveys in which young people are asked to list matters that concern them most. In such surveys, personal issues far outweigh general social issues as matters of concern to teenagers.

Shifting Concerns

The nationwide Gallup Youth surveys, in which a representative sample of teenagers are polled, have been conducted several times since 1977. The surveys give us a picture not only of what young people are anxious about, but also of how these anxieties have changed over the past two decades.

In 1989, for example, 60 percent of the teenagers in a nationwide sample named drug abuse as the most serious problem facing them. This figure was up from 35 percent in 1983 and 27 percent in 1977. Peer pressure was the next most frequently mentioned problem, with 13 percent of the teens listing it as the most serious issue. There was a slight decrease in the percentage of teenagers who ranked alcohol abuse and teenage pregnancy as the most serious problems of youth.

A new concern which emerged in the 1989 survey did not appear in earlier samplings. For the first time, 3 percent of the teenagers contacted listed teenage gangs as the most serious problem facing their age group. Only 1 percent of the teens surveyed cited suicide as the biggest issue facing them.

An unexpected finding was the drop in the number of teenagers who listed the generation gap as the most serious problem they faced. In 1977, 20 percent of teens surveyed put parent-child conflicts at the top of their list, while only 1 percent of the teenagers placed such problems first in the 1989 survey.

Although it did not appear in the Gallup survey, an abiding concern of many teenagers I talk with is the divorce — real or imagined — of their parents. Even for teenagers whose parents are happily married, divorce is still a concern because so many of their friends' parents are divorced.

What Parents Can Do

Perhaps the most important thing we can do to help teenagers is to take their anxieties and concerns seriously. Many young people are often reluctant to talk about their fears, trying to give the impression that they are happy and carefree when in fact they are not. What we can do is open the door for discussion — and leave it open. We can say something to the effect of "Look, I know it's hard to talk about things that are bothering you, but when you're ready to talk, I'll always be ready to listen. Okay?"

If we say it and mean it (if we are ready to be there whenever our teenager is ready to talk, and not just when we are ready to listen), the teenager will eventually talk about his or her worries when the time is right. This is much more important than it may at first seem, because discussing problems is one of the healthiest ways for teenagers to handle their anxieties.

WHY TEENS ARE SHY

Amy, at age 14, is convinced that her clothes are uncool, that the way she walks is clumsy, and that there is even something wrong with the food she eats at lunch. For her, walking into school every day is like walking onto a stage alone; she's sure that her classmates and even her teachers are examining her every move.

During early adolescence, most young people go through a period of shyness. It is an age when they develop what I call an "imaginary audience" — the belief that others are watching them and are preoccupied with their appearance and actions. Self-consciousness about the audience's approval usually decreases with age and positive social experiences. On the other hand, young people who enter adolescence with a predisposition toward shyness may become even *more* shy when "the audience" appears. And, at this age, children's fears about not measuring up to others can interfere with their ability to make friends and establish healthy relationships.

Persistent shyness often stems from childhood experiences — doing poorly in school or being compared unfavorably with other children, for example. Some children learn shyness by modeling the behavior of their shy parents. There is also evidence that extreme shyness is an inborn personality trait.

In their research on shy adolescents, Philip Zimbardo, Ph.D., and Shirley Radl found that the majority of the shy students they studied eventually mastered their shyness. The researchers described a number of techniques that these students employed to overcome their problem: making a firm resolution to initiate social interactions, identifying and analyzing those situations that were most conducive to their feeling shy, learning to be comfortable with themselves, recognizing that being alone need not lead to loneliness or feelings of inadequacy, and practicing social skills (such as asking for and listening to other people's opinions).

What Parents Can Do

It's important for us as parents to assess whether a teenager's shyness is a temporary phase triggered by circumstances, or an abiding disposition. For a small minority of teens, extreme shyness may be a sign of debilitating anxiety that requires professional help. But, the majority of teens who suffer from such anxiety can learn to overcome their shyness.

In helping them do this, we might well borrow from Carol Burnett, a shy teenager herself, who counseled her three daughters as follows:

"Other people...[are] not always evaluating and judging you in critical ways. They're thinking about themselves... You have to come out and reach out to people...The more you smile and are outgoing to people, the more you are going to get that back."

If we help teenagers appreciate that the audience they dread is largely imaginary, they can usually overcome their shyness. They will then be free to build the friendships that are so important in making a successful transition into adulthood.

IN THE EYE OF THE BEHOLDER

Attractiveness is socially reinforcing: we pay more attention to attractive people than we do to unattractive ones. And, in adolescence, attractiveness is judged first and foremost in physical terms. This helps to explain teenagers' extreme self-consciousness about their physical appearance, as well as the fact that attractive teenagers tend to have higher self-esteem and self-confidence than teens who are less physically attractive.

Influential Stereotypes

But what constitutes physical attractiveness? Although there are wide individual differences in what is considered attractive, there is societal consensus as well. In contemporary society, the ideals of attractiveness are often the reigning male and female movie stars. A decade or so ago, Robert Redford and Farrah Fawcett were widely considered as standard setters, whereas today teen idols might be Mel Gibson and Michelle Pfeiffer. Young people compare themselves to these cultural stereotypes and assess their own attractiveness according to how close they come to the ideal. They also evaluate their peers' attractiveness in the same way.

Of course, not all adolescents accept these cultural stereotypes of attractiveness. Some teenagers show their independence by choosing models of attractiveness considered idiosyncratic by the majority of their peers. Teenagers who affect the "punk" look are, among other things, showing their disdain for the conventional ideals of attractiveness. At the same time, because we give as much attention to those who are unusual as to those who are attractive, the "punkers" get more social reinforcement than if they groomed and dressed in more conventional ways.

Although concern about their physical attractiveness is a universal characteristic of adolescents as they undergo the psychological and physical metamorphosis from child to adult, this concern is multiplied in our media-conscious society. One result is that teenagers seek to enhance their appearance by wearing the "right" clothing, in the "right" condition.

In one study, teenagers were asked what they would do if, after driving to a much-anticipated party, they discovered a grease spot on their skirt or slacks. Young adolescents said they would go home, "stand in a dark place" at the party, or "spill something on themselves at the party" so the stain would look fresh. Children (who have yet to enter this difficult stage of development) and older teenagers (who, fortunately, are past this phase) were much less concerned and said things like, "They are my friends, they will understand."

What Parents Can Do

Clearly, personal appearance is important. We parents can encourage our teenagers to learn good hygiene, and to dress and groom themselves so as to give the best possible impression. We can also help adolescents who deviate from the societal norms of attractiveness to make the most of what they have, by wearing attractive hairstyles and clothing that — in cut and color — accentuate the young person's strong points.

Emotional and psychological support is also important. Young men who are below the norm for height should be reminded of successful movie stars of small stature, such as Dustin Hoffman, Dudley Moore, and Michael J. Fox. One girl very concerned about her freckles was reassured when she learned that Cleopatra, the queen of the Nile, had freckles, too.

Most importantly, we need to teach our children the fundamental truth of appearance and attractiveness: we all end up getting the face we deserve. Eventually, our personality shows through, and the physically attractive man or woman who is bitter and hateful will look the part. In the same way, the plainest-looking person who is good and decent will have a face that others find eye-catching and charming. Over time, if we help our teen to be as good a person as possible, his or her appearance will become attractive all by itself.

EATING DISORDERS

There was no resemblance whatsoever between the girl who had been described to me as a tall, pretty honor student, and the emaciated person who looked up at me from the hospital bed. Carol was being fed intravenously to keep her alive, after she had gone from a weight of 120 pounds to 85 pounds. She was suffering from *anorexia nervosa*, an emotional disorder characterized by self-starvation with a resultant loss of 25 percent or more of body weight. An estimated 6 to 10 percent of anorexics literally die of starvation.

Anorexia and a closely related illness — bulimia (a pattern of gorging on high-caloric foods and then dieting severely or inducing vomiting) — are most often found in intelligent, accomplished, and attractive young women from affluent families. The prime period for the appearance of these disorders is generally between the ages of 12 and 19, but they are also found in older women and in younger girls. Although only about 1 in 100 young women in the prime age group actually develops anorexia or bulimia, recent studies suggest that close to 20 percent exhibit at least one symptom of an eating disorder. Symptoms include excessive dieting and an obsessive concern with weight and weighing oneself, as well as the arbitrary elimination of some foods from the daily diet.

Who and Why

Many young women who develop anorexia and bulimia have a characteristic personality syndrome. This often begins with a pattern of perfectionism and high achievement at school, combined with an excessive "goodness" at home, all of which seem to derive from the extraordinary need of some girls to please their parents. When these girls reach adolescence, they come to resent their lack of independence but are unable to give up the "good girl" image and rebel against their parents. Anorexia allows a young woman to assert herself passively against her parents, who feel helpless in the face of her illness. At the same time, it also gives the young woman a feeling of being in control of her own impulses — a feeling that helps compensate for her low sense of self-esteem.

Another factor contributing to the development of these disorders is the adolescent's preoccupation with appearance and attractiveness. Indeed, many anorexics and bulimics seem to exaggerate greatly the connection between weight and attractiveness. Carol had been rejected by a boy she had dated, and she was sure this was because she was too fat, even though she had never been excessively overweight. Shortly thereafter, Carol began limiting her food intake. At the same time, however, she began preparing elaborate, high-caloric meals for her family.

Most young people go through a period of intense preoccupation with their appearance in early adolescence. To enhance their appearance, some boys go on a regime of exercise (such as weight lifting), while girls are more likely to go on diets. For the majority of teenagers, however, this excessive concern with physical appearance is a phase that usually ends by middle to late adolescence.

What Parents Can Do

When an adolescent fits the "model child" personality pattern, and excessive concern with appearance persists or the teenager shows more than one of the symptoms described above, parents should be alert to the possibility of anorexia or bulimia. Inasmuch as the teen is emotionally convinced that she is too fat, rational arguments that she is too thin and is endangering her health will have no effect. In fact, by showing concern and distress, parents reinforce the behavior pattern.

As hard as it is, parents have to avoid talking about or paying special attention to the teenager's appearance or eating habits. Nor should parents excuse the teen from her homework, lessons, or household chores. Instead, parents should emphasize the young woman's talents and abilities, and reward her for taking on age-appropriate responsibilities. By acting in this way, parents eliminate any of the "secondary gains" the young woman might obtain from her behavior, and so weaken her motivation for engaging in it.

If these measures do not work, and you feel that your teenager might develop full-blown anorexia or bulimia, you should seek professional counseling. Either of the organizations listed below can provide you with guidance in this regard. Anorexia and bulimia are severe illnesses, which are more easily and effectively treated if they are detected early.

To obtain more information, write or call:

ANAD (National Association of Anorexia Nervosa and Associated Disorders), P.O. Box 7, Highland Park, IL 60035, (312) 831-3438.

American Anorexia/Bulimia Association, Inc., 133 Cedar Lane, Teaneck, NJ 07666, (201) 836-1800.

ACTIVITY OVERLOAD

"He's not even used to his size-eleven shoes," a mother confided in me recently, "but he is doing tennis, guitar, the school newspaper, and still getting A's. I think it's too much, but he enjoys it all and doesn't want to give anything up. What should I do?"

My answer to this mother is the same as it is to all parents with this "problem:" "Don't insist on your son's giving up any of his activities, and communicate that you can live with this hectic schedule if he can. Tell him how much you admire and appreciate all that he is doing — and doing well, but that you will love and admire him just as much if he chooses to drop one or more activities."

Patterns of Self-Actualization

Able young people have a very strong need to develop the many facets of their personalities. As long as this self-actualization — the attempt to realize one's potential — is not overdone, it can be productive and healthy. On the other hand, if the teenager appears harried and frazzled, or if important work is left undone or done too quickly and poorly, then the young person is probably over-scheduled.

Some teenagers show no outward signs of being stressed by a crowded schedule of activities, but may still not benefit from such a regimen. In my clinical work, I have encountered two patterns of active involvement that may not have positive long-term outcomes.

One of these I call the "easy rider" syndrome. For young people who exhibit this pattern, everything comes much too easily. They can sit down at a piano and play a song without ever having taken a lesson. And, they can get good grades with little more than a cursory scan of a textbook the night before an exam. These types of teenagers may never acquire the motivation to work hard at anything in particular, and they need to be strongly encouraged to concentrate their energies and make a commitment to a few major pursuits.

The other potentially unhealthy pattern of self-actualization is what I call the "lonely idol" syndrome. These teenagers seem to have it all: they are top students, good athletes, social leaders, and a credit to their families, churches, and communities. Everyone looks up to them and admires them, so they are sought out by their peers for advice and counsel. The only problem is that many "lonely idol" teenagers feel they cannot confide any of their own problems, concerns, and anxieties to anyone else. Often, such young people feel isolated and alone, but they are committed to presenting the image of perfection. It is not unusual for young people of the "lonely idol" type to develop severe depressive reactions.

What Parents Can Do

If your teenager is heavily scheduled, the first thing to do is assess the situation correctly and determine if the schedule is a healthy or unhealthy one. The most important clue in this regard is whether or not your teenager is really enjoying and thriving. Secondly, does he or she have a sense of humor, including the ability to step back and laugh at himself or herself? If your teenager is having a good time and demonstrates a robust sense of humor, you really do not have to worry about his or her busy schedule.

On the other hand, when young people take themselves, their responsibilities, and their image too seriously, there is reason for concern. At such times, it is appropriate to tell teenagers how much we love and admire them, and that we will love them even more if they will do a little less.

Adolescents who have the ability to do many things well want to realize their talents and abilities. And, we should certainly encourage and support this self-actualization. Unfortunately, a blessing can sometimes become a curse, and that is when we need to intervene and ensure that self-actualization does not become self-destruction.

DEPRESSION

I had given it all I had, but it was still Leslie who was on the stage receiving the award, rather than me. Not being very athletic, I found my competitive outlet in oratory. My only real rival for representing our high school in the city finals was Leslie, a thin, scrawny kid with — unfortunately — a strong and powerful voice. I had gone over my speech again and again, practicing every nuance and gesture for maximum effect. I was sure I had it just right. But, the judges gave Leslie higher marks on all counts.

I knew all the standard consolations, like "Winning isn't everything," but I felt miserable and was sure my life was all downhill from that moment on. When, a few weeks later, one of my poems was published in the school paper, life seemed a lot brighter — particularly since Leslie had never had anything published. Ha!

The Psychology of Depression

Depression is part of our human condition. In extreme cases, it can lead to chronic apathy, withdrawal, and suicide, but there is also a "normal" range of depressive reactions we should be alert for.

The main psychological ingredients of depression are attachment and loss. Whenever we become attached to a person, place, or thing, we also take the risk of losing it. Some young children who are moved from foster home to foster home will no longer attach to adults. Having already attached to several different sets of caretakers, they refuse to do it anymore, because they experience too much pain when they have to separate from those to whom they have bonded. We also grow attached to places, which is why we may feel depressed when we have to move to a new home or see a neighborhood we have known and enjoyed become run-down. And, we become attached to things, like money and possessions, which can lead to depression if they are lost.

In addition, we may become attached to our mental constructions of people, places, and things. As described in the section on teenage shyness, young people create an "imaginary audience," which they believe is observing and judging them. They are very concerned about not losing the audience's positive regard, and they may become depressed when they believe that the audience is privy to their embarrassment.

Imagined places can have the same sort of impact. Part of my depression at losing the oratory contest was over not going to the state competitions, which I mentally pictured as being wildly glamorous. In a similar way, our attachment to things can also become much too intense because of personal need. Some teenagers over-invest emotionally in possessions, such as a car, a piece of clothing, or jewelry, so that when these things are lost, life does not seem worth living.

What Parents Can Do

We should be alert for signs of depression whenever there is significant loss in a teenager's life. Such losses include the death of grandparents, the divorce of parents, moving to a new city and school, the breakup of a relationship, and even losing an important athletic competition. While we cannot know for sure just how depressed such an event will make the young person, some depression is inevitable. This may appear not only as low mood and apathy, but also as aggressive surliness.

If we know that a teenager has experienced a significant loss, we need to give him or her the opportunity to talk about the feelings that result. And, it is important to communicate even with those teenagers who seem unable to talk about their feelings. We need to say something to the effect that "while I cannot know exactly how you are feeling, I know that it hurts a lot, and I wish there were something I could do to ease the pain." Explain that though it is very hard to accept now, the pain will ease with time.

In other words, when a teenager is depressed, we should behave in the same manner as we would with our spouse, our relatives, and our friends. We should provide understanding, support, and a readiness to listen.

CHALLENGES TO SELF-ESTEEM

Walking around a suburban high school campus last spring, I observed an attractive young woman descending the stairs from the main entrance. A young man saw her and began to smile. As he approached her, he said, "Hi Sheila," in a friendly voice. The young woman simply ignored him and continued on her way. The smile disappeared from the young man's face as he turned and walked slowly in the other direction, looking down at his feet. I could see the color rising in his neck as he moved away.

The Cruelest Cuts

Having a friendly overture rejected is just one of the many experiences that can make a teenager feel "down on himself." This is particularly true for those teenagers who already feel insecure and have a low opinion of themselves. Such teenagers are apt to perceive unprovoked rejection or ridicule as something they themselves have somehow encouraged or initiated. This misinterpretation, in turn, reinforces a young person's negative self-image.

Other teenagers are sometimes hard on themselves because they set very high — often unrealistic — standards or goals. They have to receive all A's, or win every tennis match, or stick to a strict exercise or diet regimen. When they fail to achieve these inflated goals, they can be very self-critical and feel that they have made a mess of things. If your child is this sort of teen, it is important to let them know that perfection is definitely *not* the norm in the real, adult world.

Like most adults, teenagers feel annoyed when they make human mistakes; for instance, when they thoughtlessly say something hurtful, or when they are clumsy and break or spill something, particularly in public. Teenagers want to think well of themselves and to believe that they are effectively managing themselves and the events in their lives. When teenagers say something thoughtless, their feelings of self-esteem and their belief that they are coping well are affected. "How could I *say* that?" one young teen wondered after blurting out, "That's dumb!" to his teacher in front of his entire history class.

Although teenagers can be hard on themselves, they tend to bounce back pretty quickly. Most adolescents have a fairly good opinion of their abilities, and their down moods are usually temporary. Following a setback like the one described above, most teenagers will work harder or attempt some new strategies.

What Parents Can Do

The way to respond to our teenager's self-deprecating moods depends on both the teenager and on the specific situation. Teenagers who are upset with themselves because of some failure need help putting the experience into perspective. They need to be reminded of all that they have accomplished, and all the successes that they will have in the future. And, when they feel they have acted stupidly or said something "dumb," it is always helpful for us to tell them of the many stupid things we ourselves have done in the past — and overcome.

We can also prepare adolescents for the inevitable down experiences by spontaneously saying good things about them. When we occasionally tell our teenager that he or she is a good person, and that other people — such as a teacher or coach — share this opinion, we help to diminish the feelings of self-deprecation that are likely to occur when all-too-human mistakes are made.

COPING WITH STRESS

Whenever I visit high schools, I make it a practice to have lunch with a small group of students. At one such luncheon, a high school senior told me that she had three to four hours of homework each night and inquired, "Isn't that stressing me?" In response, I asked whether her homework was read and corrected, and she allowed that it was. I also asked whether she had time in study halls during the day to get some of the work done, and again she agreed that this was the case. I then handed down my unwelcome verdict: "No, you are not being stressed; it is not too much meaningful, constructive homework for a high school senior."

In the broadest sense, stress is any demand for adaptation and is therefore a constant part of life. But, we usually use "stress" in the more narrow sense of an extraordinary demand for adaptation. What is extraordinary for one person, however, may not be out of the ordinary for another. Three or four hours of homework, for example, would indeed be stressful if the student I spoke to was in the second or third grade. The degree to which we are stressed by any event depends partly on the event and partly on us.

Causes and Effects of Stress

Although each generation has its own set of stressors, I believe that contemporary teenagers are under more stress than, say, young people who were teenagers in the late 1940's or the 1950's.

Teenagers today have more freedom to travel, to be sexually active, and to use drugs than was true for earlier generations. Likewise, teenagers today experience more loss than in the past. This is largely attributable to the high divorce rate in this country. At least 40 percent of American adolescents have experienced divorce by the age of 18. In addition, because of the tremendous emphasis on academic achievement and economic competition, academic failure looms as a more important stressor than in the past.

Stress burns up energy. When we are under constant stress, we use more energy than we can replenish with food and rest, and we may begin to show physical symptoms such as fatigue, headaches, and stomachaches. If the stress persists, more serious problems can result, as stress can also contribute to the exacerbation of other illnesses. Because stress affects our health, it also affects our performance, and teenagers who are under constant stress will begin to do poorly at school and may lose interest completely in extracurricular activities.

Stress is also an unpleasant experience, so teenagers may attempt to ease the pain the same way adults do — with the aid of drugs or alcohol. But, this temporary relief is purchased at the price of the increased stress associated with the hazards of drug and alcohol abuse.

What Parents Can Do

We can't eliminate many of the stressors teenagers face today, but we can help them cope more effectively by talking with them on a regular basis. Talking helps people explore alternatives and is one of the most important ways of dealing with stress. During conversations about stressful situations, we should try to consider what our teenagers are saying from their perspective, as well as from our own. This allows us to be more helpful and less judgmental.

Talking is an especially important means of coping with the stress of loss. Many teenagers tell me the most hurtful thing about their parents' divorce was that they were not told until it happened, and that even then they were given little opportunity to express their feelings. Because of the prevalence of divorce, teenagers worry about whether their parents are going to stay together. We should appreciate these concerns, and when we parents have a particularly emotional argument, it is important to let our teenager know that it is just a disagreement which will not break up our marriage.

Talking is also important in helping a teenager cope with failure. Losing a game or doing badly on a test does not seem so awful, if a teenager talks about it with someone who can help put the experience in perspective. Talk is indeed cheap, but it can also be very valuable.

GRADUATION FROM CHILDHOOD

Occasionally, on Halloween, I encounter a tall ghost at my door. Hidden behind the sheet and mask is a young teenager not quite ready to give up one of the rituals usually reserved for children. There are, in fact, quite a number of habits, rituals, and practices — unique to childhood and adolescence — that must be given up in the progress toward adulthood. Letting go of these prerogatives is not always easy, as the tall ghosts repeatedly remind me.

Adolescents, like younger children, enjoy a number of liberties with respect to dress, language, and behavior that they will no longer be granted once they are adults. Teenagers, in effect, possess a social license that expires once they enter adulthood. And, it is a license that for many young people expires too soon.

To make it easier for teenagers to relinquish the prerogatives of childhood and adolescence, society has provided a number of rituals and ceremonies. One of the most important of these transition ceremonies is graduation, and many high schoolers approach this impending occasion with mixed emotions.

One Last Fling

Graduations are important because participation in them is a public acceptance of students' changing status and the new, more demanding limits of adult life. While young people welcome the new freedom and independence they gain as adults, they may also mourn the sense of comfort and security inherent in the knowledge that their parents — and the larger society — were there to set limits and boundaries for them.

Consequently, during this time of change, they may eat too much or very little, and sleep more or less than usual. High school seniors may concentrate less on their studies and more on having fun during their last semester — all in an effort to enjoy one last exercise of the freedoms and privileges of adolescence, before assuming the responsibilities of adulthood. If and when they go away to college, recent high school graduates are likely to call home frequently, complaining about everything from the quality of the food to their living quarters and roommates.

What Parents Can Do

If we appreciate the stress we ourselves encounter in making transitions — to new jobs, new living arrangements, and new relationships — we can be more sympathetic to the experiences our children go through as they make the transition to adulthood. We can excuse their occasional regressions to childlike behavior, such as stubbornness, inappropriate demands, and insensitivity. We may even find it easier to accept the minor acts of defiance, such as forgetting to return the car keys, leaving the house improperly dressed, and refusing to eat foods served at the family table.

It is also not unheard of for us parents to regress when we have to deal with our son's or daughter's departure from our home. We may try to re-establish limits more suited to a younger child, perhaps because we wish to be needed again. Like our children, we have to realize that giving up the prerogatives associated with childhood and adolescence is one of life's necessary losses. We help young people best when we sympathize with their loss, while we also encourage them to move forward into maturity.

2
FRIENDSHIP AND DATING

OVERVIEW

Friends have significant roles to play at many age levels, but they are particularly important during adolescence. At this stage, they serve as "transitional objects" of a sort, helping teenagers separate from their parents and prepare for other long-term emotional commitments.

The "transitional" nature of adolescent friendships in no way diminishes their importance. It is through friendships that teenagers learn to take responsibility, provide support, and give their loyalty to non-family members. It is also in teenage friendships that young people find confidants with whom to share thoughts and feelings that they are not comfortable sharing with their parents. Such sharing becomes one of the elements of true intimacy, which will be established later.

Dating is also both important and transitional, as it is the conventional way that young men and women begin to break down the barriers between the sexes that were created during childhood. Usually, dating comes towards the middle or end of adolescence, after teenagers have established solid, same-sex relationships. Dating patterns, however, tend to be rather faddish and vary with time and place. During the 1970's, for example, dating was not popular, but it seems to have regained its appeal in the 1990's. Likewise, in some communities young people begin dating as pre-teens, while in other communities dating is not common until after a teenager reaches the age of 16.

Although patterns of dating seem to be cyclical, patterns of sexual activity are not. Before mid-century, relatively few teenagers were sexually active. Now, as we approach the end of the century, the majority of adolescents are sexually active. This fact has changed the emotional landscape of adolescence, presenting difficult, new problems for parents and teenagers. Today, unlike a half century ago, pregnancy and venereal disease are real threats to a significant number of teens.

In general, teenage friendships with members of either sex are healthy and worthwhile, and a lack of friends may be an indication of other problems. Sometimes, however, we parents may not approve of our teenager's friends, and we need to examine our reasons for this negative reaction carefully. Often, the reasons have more to do with our personal preferences than logical concerns about our teenager. In a similar manner, we often overestimate the influence of a peer group on our teenager. While the peer group is most influential in matters of taste and preference, we parents are most influential in more abiding matters of standards, beliefs, and values.

Even when a teenager has incorporated our beliefs and values, he or she may not always be in control of the situation. This is particularly true at parties, which can sometimes grow very much out of control. That's why we need to make sure that any party our teenager attends has an adult present in the background, and that alcohol and other drugs are not available.

As our adolescent's interest in the opposite sex increases, one result may be feelings of unattractiveness and inferiority. We need to be understanding when teenagers feel this way, and do what we can to help them feel better about themselves. This is especially important when a relationship our teen has been involved in "breaks up." We need to appreciate how painful this may be, and reassure our teen that we are on his or her side.

Although teenagers usually have a good understanding of themselves and of social interactions, they still sometimes need our help and guidance. For example, we should be ready to help when an adolescent either gives or receives a gift that is inappropriate because of its content or cost. And, our guidance is particularly important in regard to the sexual aspects of a teen's social life. At an earlier time, when most teenagers were not sexually active, we parents could get away with a brief talk about the birds and the bees, or just giving our teen a book. No longer. Today, we have to overcome our reluctance and talk openly with teens about sexual matters. This point will be made in a number of different contexts in this chapter, because adolescents need information and advice about various aspects of sexuality.

One particularly unfortunate aspect of the increased sexual activity among teens is an apparent increase in date rape. While we cannot prevent such assaults entirely, we can teach our teenage sons and daughters how to minimize the possibility of date rape. We also need to make sure they are informed about the dramatic increase in sexually transmitted diseases among young people. As parents, it is our responsibility to educate our teenagers about these diseases, their effects, and how to avoid them.

Regrettably, we cannot rely on sex education programs in the schools — which are often ineffective — to do this sort of work for us. This is especially true in regard to advising teenagers who are already sexually active. Rather than simply accepting teenage sexual activity as a reality we just have to live with, we need to do all we can to ensure that a sexually active teenager accepts the responsibilities which comes with this new freedom.

In dealing with teenage friendships, dating, and sexual activity, there are a few goals worth keeping in mind. While we want to encourage teenage friendships, we also want to help adolescents learn to choose wisely — to know when and when not to enter into a relationship. With respect to dating and sexual activity, our goal should be to have a frank and ongoing discourse about sexual activity with our teenager. In this way, we progress toward the broader goal of raising a young person who is knowledgeable, responsible, and compassionate in his or her love life.

WHAT FRIENDSHIP MEANS TO TEENS

"But if I couldn't be a member of the Society Six, I was delighted to be accepted into the next group on the social scale, a larger and more fluid one, ten or fifteen girls, democratic enough at least to be nameless..." writes Susan Allen Toth in her book *Blooming: A Small-town Girlhood.* "Most of us were moderately attractive, but one or two of us didn't date at all for years. Most of us were 'popular,' but I don't know exactly why. Perhaps we merely defined ourselves in relation to the Society Six and to all the other girls below us, the loners, the stupid ones, the fat ones. We had absorbed already by sixth grade a set of careful and cruel distinctions."

As this quotation suggests, friendships in pre-adolescence and adolescence serve a very different purpose than they do in childhood. Friendships in childhood are usually a matter of chance, whereas in adolescence they are most often a matter of choice. Children's friendships center on activities and the peers who happen to live nearby, go to the same school, or be on the same sports teams. Adolescents, in contrast, choose their friends on the basis of status, common interests, and similar values, as well as personality similarities and differences.

Functions of Adolescent Friendships

The major purpose of adolescent friendships is to provide the young people with transitional emotional attachments, which enable them to separate and attain independence from their parents. Teenagers begin to look to their friends for the understanding, support, and guidance they once sought from their mothers and fathers. And, when teens complain that their parents "just don't understand them," the clear implication is that their friends do.

A second function of adolescent friendships, well-illustrated in Toth's quotation, is to help teenagers define their social status. There are usually three or four general social groupings in a high school, which reflect the major social strata of adolescents. At this stage, teens begin to define themselves as "jocks," "brains," "socials," or "baddies," according to their peer group.

Still a third function of adolescent friendships is to prepare young people for heterosexual relationships. In early adolescence, teenagers often establish what psychiatrist Harry Stack Sullivan called *chumships*. These same-sex friendships are often quite intense and involve a great deal of sharing of likes, dislikes, and confidences. Because of the intensity of these relationships, teenagers involved in chumships can become quite jealous of their chums and resent sharing them with others. In Sullivan's view, young people who have successfully dealt with the intimacies and conflicting emotions of chumships are better prepared for later heterosexual relationships than teens who have not had chums.

We need to remember, however, that teenagers differ in their social needs. Some young people require a large number of friends and a busy social calendar to feel happy and fulfilled. Other teenagers are content with a few close friends and occasional social outings. Often, teenagers in the same family will be quite different with respect to their social lifestyles. There is no right or wrong, or good or bad, in these differences.

What Parents Can Do

As parents, we have to be supportive of teenage friendships, even when the friends seem to be taking over many of the functions we once performed. (This does not mean, however, that we should not intervene when the friendship is a destructive or unhealthy one.) We also have to be sensitive to individual differences in sociability. If our teenager does not have as many friends as we might like, we have to understand this as the pattern that works for him or her, even if it isn't right for us. Pushing a teenager socially is likely to backfire, achieving the reverse of its intended effect. In the end, a teenager's choice of friends is his or her individual path to independence, and we help most by respecting the path that is chosen.

There are, however, teenagers who would like to make and have more friends, but may not be able to do so for a variety of reasons. Perhaps the most common reason is shyness, which may inhibit an adolescent from initiating interactions that might lead to friendships. It is helpful to encourage shy teens to talk more with family members, the clerk at the supermarket, and so on, so as to develop more self-confidence in their ability to converse.

We should also encourage shy teens to take the initiative and not wait for other people to do so. We need to help these teens understand that their phone calls are likely to be welcomed and will please other teenagers. Too often, shy teens fail to appreciate that their calls can have the same effect on other teens that the calls of others have on them.

WHOSE FRIEND IS SHE, ANYWAY?

"My best friend's parents are really messed up, and my mom and dad don't think that I should see her. What have her parents' problems got to do with her and me? My parents are afraid her problems will rub off on me somehow. I told my mom we should help her, not desert her."

These remarks by a 16-year-old girl, reported in *The Private Life of the American Teenager,* by Jane Norman and Myron W. Harris, Ph.D., give voice to what may be the most common parental misconception regarding adolescent friendships: that teenagers are unduly (and almost always negatively) influenced by their peer attachments. As noted in the previous piece, most teenagers choose friends who have the same interests, values, and beliefs that they themselves do. Such friends are unlikely to change a teenager's morals or influence the teen in a negative way. And, although we often think otherwise, influence is always a two-way street — our children are as likely to affect their friends as their friends are apt to influence them.

Of course, some teenagers do choose their friends for reasons other than common interests. One overweight young man told me that he befriends "misfits" because they are the only ones who accept him as an equal; they do not tease or make fun of him, since they know what it feels like to be taunted and ostracized. Other teenagers may choose friends who have traits that they feel they lack. For example, a shy young man may befriend the class leader. Although such friendships may serve a purpose for both parties, they tend to be short-lived.

What Parents Can Do

In the previous piece, I discussed the general role played by adolescent friendships. Here, I want to focus on the functions served by individual friendships. Yet, in most cases, the guidelines for parents are much the same — namely, we should not intervene in our teenager's choice of friends. This is true even when the friend's dress or habits make us cringe. When we are tempted to say something negative about our teenager's friends, we need to think back to some of our own teenage companions and our parents' reactions to them. I recall how unhappy I felt when my mother was brusque with one of my closest friends. That memory, in turn, helped me to be reasonably hospitable to some of the "characters" my own sons brought home.

We should step in, however, when a relationship is destructive or denies a teenager the right to make his or her own choices. For example, our teen may unknowingly befriend an adolescent alcoholic who, in turn, may encourage frequent consumption of alcohol. In such a case, we need to tell our teen that the friendship must be terminated before it leads to serious problems.

Fortunately, in most cases teenagers' friends are fine. Our negative reaction to some of them may, in fact, be the product of our own separation anxiety. When our children show signs of growing up and developing attachments outside the family, we parents may feel scared and depressed. There is, however, a positive side to our teenagers' new relationships, and that is the one we need to focus on. We should take pleasure and pride in the fact that we have done a good job as parents, having reared a young person who is able to give and receive one of life's great gifts — friendship.

PEER GROUPS — BLESSING OR CURSE?

"Chum Moo Do!" I said. "Sounds like something you would order at a Chinese restaurant!" To this, my son calmly replied, "Chung Moo Do, Dad, and it is a Korean martial arts program that I have enrolled in. It is a cooperative system, and everyone tries to help everyone else. The Master says that you learn from helping others and that others learn from helping you." "Who is this master?" I asked, a little rattled. "Remember, there is one and only one God, and don't you forget it." To which my son answered, just loud enough for me to hear, "And we all know who that is."

I cite this personal example to emphasize a point made earlier in this chapter — that an adolescent tends to find a peer group which shares the same values and moral standards. That is why it is so important, especially when our children are young, for us to be as clear and as consistent as we can — in both our words and our actions — about our values and standards. If we do this, our children can internalize those moral guidelines and use them as a bulwark against unhealthy influences in adolescence.

Unhealthy Peer Groups

There are times when an adolescent may be vulnerable to joining a peer group that does not really reflect his or her basic values: for instance, if the family has moved and the teenager has to start at a new high school. Under such circumstances, it is sometimes very difficult to be immediately accepted into existing groups, and the teen may seek support in groups that are easier to join but do not reflect his or her values.

Once a teenager is identified as part of a particular group, it is very difficult to change affiliations. A teenage client of mine befriended a girl who was in a group known as the "baddies" or "hoods." This group did not really represent my client's values, but her judgment was clouded by the fact that her parents were divorcing, and she accepted the friendship for the wrong reasons.

After going to a party where she was ridiculed for not smoking pot, she realized what she had gotten into. She also came to appreciate that her reputation was colored by the group she was with. At that point, she tried to join a different group. Not only was she rejected by the new group, but her "friends" in the "hood" group began circulating damaging stories about her.

What Parents Can Do

Forewarned is forearmed. If we know that our teenager is at risk for getting involved with the wrong group, there are actions we can take. First and foremost, we need to talk with our teen and acknowledge that some circumstances — such as death, divorce, or relocation — can be hurtful, so it is natural to feel resentful and angry. We need to say that we are sorry that he or she is hurting, and if the cause was in whole or part anything we did, it was not intended to cause pain or embarrassment. We then must make an ongoing

effort to help the adolescent deal with the stress of the hurtful events, so he or she will be less likely to seek out peer
groups that are supportive for the wrong reasons.

If our teenager does get in with the wrong group, for
whatever reason, there are still steps we can take. The most
radical, of course, is for the teenager to switch to a different
school. That was what my client and her parents decided
should happen. Another approach is to help the teenager
become involved in groups outside of school, such as those
organized by a church or synagogue. These groups fulfill
the need for peer group identification, and give the teenager the security and self-confidence which make it easier to
become part of an appropriate in-school peer group.

We shouldn't be too hard on teenagers when they choose
the wrong friends; we have all made this mistake. The important thing is to help young people reflect upon — and
gain some insight into — the reasons for their choice of
friends. Such understanding is the best insurance against
making the same mistake twice.

YOUR TEEN IS
INVITED TO A PARTY!

"I was at this party, and my boyfriend kept giving me beer. I got so wasted! Then, I got really sick in front of everyone and made a complete fool of myself. I'm so embarrassed!"

Teenage parties present a difficult problem for parents. On the one hand, we want our teenagers to know that we trust them and recognize their growing independence. On the other hand, we also know — as the above anecdote illustrates — that unsupervised parties can quickly grow out of control.

For adolescents, parties provide an opportunity to socialize and let off steam. In a way, parties also offer teens a support group. But, whether your teenager is throwing or attending a party, some ground rules have to be set.

The most important rule is that there must be some adult supervision. Knowing that there are adults around can help teenagers stay in control and can also keep out uninvited guests.

What Parents Can Do

If your teenager is attending a party, you need to call the host's parents to ensure that they will be there to chaperon. Be prepared, however, for a battle with your teen over this phone call. Here's a typical situation: Your teen says that he's going to a party on Saturday night. You ask, "Whose party?" He names a family you've never heard of. You ask, "Will his parents be there?" Your son says, "Yes." You say, "I'm going to call them to make sure." Your son says that he'll run away from home if you do this.

You can sympathize with your child, agreeing that this may seem harsh, but point out that parties can easily grow out of control. Also, remind him that as a parent, you have the right to make sure that there will be supervision. You can add something like, "Look, your friend's parents may not even know that he's having a party. Why don't you check with your friend before I call?"

If your teen is hosting a party, keep in mind that you must be sensitive to his or her standing with her peers — in other words, don't make your presence too obvious. You needn't be in the same room, or even in the same part of the house. However, you should be aware of what's going on, so you can make sure a second basic party rule is observed: no alcohol or drugs can be served, and no sexual activity is allowed.

For example, if from the second-floor landing, you suddenly notice that the party has fallen strangely silent and all the lights have been turned off, you need to investigate the situation. But, do give your child and his or her friends a chance to break it up on their own. You can accomplish this by yelling — from the top of the stairs — something like, "Hey, you guys, let's have some of those lights back on."

Your teenager will probably not like any of the rules you set for parties. On a deeper level, however, adolescents know that we set these rules because we care. And, it is our caring, rather than the rules and limits we set, that our teens will remember and appreciate long after the party is over.

THE BIRDS AND THE BEES

As my oldest son approached adolescence, I began to prepare myself to talk with him about this new stage in his life. It turned out to be one of the many tasks of parenthood for which being a child psychologist had not prepared me. Nor could I rely on experience. My father never discussed the topic with me. Ours being a joke-telling family, becoming a man meant progressive exposure to sexual ribaldry. I literally laughed my way into puberty.

Clearly, this would not do for my son. I tried initiating the discussion several times, and the first time was dismissed with an amused, "Oh, Dad, are you going to tell me about the birds and the bees?" I ended up going to the bookstore and finding an illustrated book for young teenage boys that handled the subject frankly, but in an age-appropriate way. My son accepted the book with haughty disdain, but a few years later I came upon it — rumpled and worn and obviously much read.

The Difficulty of Sex Education

While my "bibliotherapy" approach may have worked in the past, it would not suffice today. Over the past two decades, sexual language and activity has become increasingly more explicit in movies, TV shows, rock videos, and rock lyrics. Yet, even with this early exposure to sexual language and activity — and our new openness about these subjects — it is still difficult to talk with adolescents about their sexual behavior.

Why should sexuality prove so troublesome to talk about, especially in light of "the sexual revolution?" According to Freud, when children are young they are subject to the Oedipus and Electra complexes: the son is attracted to his mother, and the daughter is attracted to her father. The father therefore becomes the son's rival, and the mother is regarded as the daughter's competitor.

These triangles are resolved vicariously by the age of 5 or 6, when children identify with the parent of the same sex. However, Freud also believed that as young people become adolescent, the Oedipus and Electra complexes are reawakened and become more threatening, because the teenager is now capable of a sexual relationship. So, the teen must strongly repress this revived sexual attraction to the parent of the opposite sex. Any discussion about sexuality with the parent of the same sex is embarrassing and anxiety provoking, because it brings up these unconscious and uncomfortable feelings.

What Parents Can Do

How can parents overcome these obstacles and help a teenager adapt successfully to his or her sexuality? In this regard, I think many parents make the same two mistakes that I did. First, I assumed that sex education should be provided at the time my son was about to enter puberty. Meaningful discussions about sexual behavior, however, can and should begin much earlier. It is important to give children the correct terms for sexual organs and to avoid threats, even in jest. A woman whom we had hired as a baby-sitter once said to my young son that if he wet himself again, she would cut off his "widdler!"

Talking with children about sexual scenes on TV or in the movies provides a chance to deal with sexuality in a non-threatening way. We can use this material to help young people discriminate between casual sexual activity and that which is an outgrowth of a caring relationship.

As our teenager approaches puberty, we need to have a number of direct talks about sexual matters. Here is where I made my second mistake. I assumed that what I had to do was explain the "mechanical" details of sexual activity. In fact, the most important message we can give our teenagers is that sexual activity is part of caring, sharing, and loving — it is not an isolated act.

We need to emphasize that while sexual activity can be a very enjoyable experience, it also entails responsibilities and risks. We should explain that sexual activity is most pleasurable — and most rewarding — when it is part of an intimate relationship. Because this kind of relationship is really not possible before late adolescence, it makes sense to delay sexual activity until that time. Some things, we ought to reassure our teenager, are worth waiting for.

A HEALTHY INTEREST

Attending a high school in southern California was something of a culture shock for a short, fat Jewish boy from Detroit. When my parents decided to move to Los Angeles after I completed junior high school, I was excited at the prospect. And, though I was prepared for the glistening California sunshine, I was not prepared for the legions of tall, tanned, blond, and good-looking teenagers who filled the corridors and classrooms of Dorsey High.

In Detroit, I was able to compensate for my physical limitations with my bookishness. A broken-voiced recital of "How do I love thee? Let me count the ways..." was my counter-offensive to the height and huskiness of the football players. But, in California, if you didn't have a car, a fabulous body, or a Hollywood connection, you were out. I didn't date, not because I didn't care to, but rather because I didn't dare to!

I was soon befriended by another young man with similar problems. Morris was tall and thin, with a hooked nose and eyes a little too close together. For more than a year and a half, we watched the beautiful people and wondered why we — with our romantic souls — had not been chosen to inhabit those bodies. Our fortunes changed, however, when Morris got his driver's license, and his father let him drive the family Cadillac!

Dynamics of Dating

These personal adolescent experiences illustrate just a few of the many reasons why some teenagers show little interest in the opposite sex and dating. Some teenagers are simply slow to mature — their bodies and interests have not yet caught up with their chronological age. Other young people may feel unattractive, even when they are not, and may be reluctant to risk rejection. Still other teenagers feel shy or socially inept. While they would like to date, they are afraid they might do or say something stupid. And, some teens are afraid to date for fear they will encounter sexual demands that they are not willing to accommodate. Finally, there are those adolescents who are simply too busy with school and extracurricular activities to have time for dating.

Researchers who have studied adolescent behavior found that the earlier teenagers begin dating and going steady, the earlier they are likely to begin having sexual relations. Furthermore, the earlier teenagers become sexually active, the more likely they are to experience difficulty in heterosexual relations as young adults. On the other hand, studies also indicate that young people who delay dating too long may become overly dependent upon their parents for their social life. The healthiest pattern is to have close same-sex friendships in childhood and early adolescence, and then gradually develop heterosexual relationships during middle and late adolescence.

What Parents Can Do

When a teenager is uninterested in the opposite sex or dating, the most important thing is to assess the situation correctly. If your teen has many same-sex friends and seems busy and happy, relax and count your blessings. His or her interest in the opposite sex will emerge — in time — on its own. With young people who feel unattractive, socially insecure, or intimidated, encourage and support only same-sex friendships at first. Such friendships are the natural and best motivation for moving into boy-girl relationships.

If you have trouble restraining yourself from badgering your teenager about starting to date, take a moment to recall your own pattern of dating. I often find that parents who are overly concerned about their teenager's delayed interest had a similar history themselves. Sometimes, we need to accept our own adolescence before we can fully accept the adolescence of our offspring.

GOING OVERBOARD ON GIFTS

One of our more endearing human traits is our need to express our love and affection through gift giving. But, because of teenagers' strong desire to be liked, they often go overboard when they buy gifts for their friends. Some buy overly expensive gifts in an effort to show the depths of their feelings. And, other teenagers err by selecting gifts that are too personal or that might be misunderstood.

Inappropriate Gifts

Kate, a modest 14-year-old, received a "Virginia Is for Lovers" T-shirt from her boyfriend when he returned from vacation. "I was mortified, and stuffed the T-shirt in the back of a drawer," she said. She never wore the shirt because she felt its message implied that she and her boyfriend were more intimate than they actually were. Usually, when a teenager gives a gift that can easily be misinterpreted, it is a result of thoughtlessness rather than bad intentions.

A gift that is too extravagant is often purchased when a teenager is so enthralled with someone that an expensive gift appears the *only* way to express the emotion. There is also the wish, only partially conscious, that the expensive gift will win the affection of the person receiving it. Yet, extravagant gifts always have strings attached — which is why they are inappropriate.

When, for example, a young woman accepts a costly piece of jewelry from a young man she is dating, she may unwittingly obligate herself to go steady with him — at least that may be *his* expectation. If she then fails to live up to the implied terms of accepting the gift, he may feel betrayed. An awkward situation or bad feelings are almost sure to result.

What Parents Can Do

Perhaps the most important guidance we can give teenagers is setting an example of thoughtful — rather than lavish — gift giving. When we choose gifts for our children with their special interests and tastes in mind, we give them a caring, thoughtful model to follow. We can also help teens set realistic spending limits by insisting that they pay for gifts with their own allowance or earnings — not by borrowing from or using up savings.

If your child does choose an inappropriate gift, you might say, "It's a nice gift, but I think Amy is such a ski buff she would prefer something she could take on next month's ski trip, instead of an expensive necklace."

If, on the other hand, your teenager receives an overly expensive or a personal gift, you can help return it in a supportive rather than rejecting way. You might suggest saying something like, "I know you want me to have something that I really enjoy, and that is why I feel comfortable telling you that what I would really like is..." If a gift is totally off-base or comes from someone barely known, your teen can simply return it with a note saying he or she cannot accept it. In such cases, the less said the better.

Ultimately, gift giving and receiving is a matter of taking into account the other person's feelings. With a little guidance from us, teenagers can learn to give and receive thoughtful gifts with taste and good grace.

BREAKING UP IS HARD TO DO

Petite brunettes used to turn me to goo. What really brought about my meltdown, however, was a low, husky voice. Lois Harris combined these two traits in an extraordinarily — to me, at any rate — curvaceous body. We met in algebra class when she asked me for some assistance with simultaneous equations. She was so pleased with the help that she even invited me to her house a couple of times, to assist her with organic chemistry, as well. Once we even "necked" a little. (In those days you were "zoned," and necking meant intimacies above the neck.)

I was in the stratosphere. My head was a never-ending Hit Parade of "It Had to Be You," and "Moonlight Becomes You." Then, *it* happened. On the way to school, I saw Lois with the unnecessarily tall and handsome captain of the football team. She looked at me and smiled, then she looked up at her companion and said something to him in that low, husky voice, at which they both laughed and proceeded to walk on. I wanted to become a black hole and disappear into the universe.

Although this experience took place long ago, and I am now entering the autumn years, I still think of Lois Harris. Sometimes, too, when I am on national television, I like to imagine that Lois Harris is watching and that she hears my silent song — the one that begins, "Who's sorry now?"

First Love

Our first love, like our first sexual experience, is something we never forget. And, it appears totally unique to us — something never experienced before and never to be experienced again by anybody. For that reason, we feel we cannot possibly communicate our feelings to anyone else, especially our parents. What, after all, do couples married for eons understand about romance and "true" love?

We tend to idealize the person we first love, perceiving him or her as the embodiment of human perfection. This type of romantic love is necessarily "blind" and inevitably leads to hurt and disillusion. It is a painful but important part of growing up.

The denouement can come in many different ways. Sometimes, it may occur in the form of a forced realization that the love was one-sided, as it did in my case. Or, it can come as a result of a bitter quarrel. And, for some, the break occurs as a mutual decision to end the relationship.

However the breakup occurs, there is always a lot of pain involved. And, it is the teenager's self-perception that suffers the most damage. The adolescent has not had sufficient experience to form a reasonably objective opinion of himself or herself. The first love does a tremendous job of ego bolstering, and unfortunately, the breakup does the opposite, leaving us feeling woefully inadequate and unattractive.

But, it is reasonable to ask, don't we all feel that way when a relationship ends, even in mid-life and later? What is so special about teenagers' feelings? The answer is that adolescents are just starting to develop a sense of personal identity. Because they are young, they have fewer established "identity supports" (husbands or wives, careers, avocations, long-term friendships) outside the relationship than do adults. Their egos are therefore more fragile than ours, and the breakup of a relationship can devastate them.

What Parents Can Do

When our teenager has gone through a romantic attachment and breakup, there are some things we should probably avoid doing, as well as things we can do to help. We should avoid making light of the breakup and assuring the young person, as I was reassured after my one-sided breakup with Lois Harris, "There are always more." I didn't want to hear that then, and I don't think teenagers want to hear it now. Nor should we try and tell our teenagers how we felt when something similar happened to us. When my older brother took this tack with me, it didn't help a bit.

As a result of my own experiences, I took a different approach when one of my sons was, as he put it, "dumped" by his girlfriend. While I did not tell him about Lois Harris, I told him what I wish I had been able to tell her. I told him that the girl was not very bright, because she was giving up an attractive, sensitive, and intelligent young man, and that she would have a hard time finding another young man who was half as good.

There is, therefore, one thing we can and should do when teenagers have been treated in a callous and thoughtless way by someone they cared for. We need to make it very clear, in our words and in our deeds, that we are on their side.

TEENS AND SEX

There is more sexual activity among teenagers today than at any other time in our history. Back in 1960, an estimated 10 percent of teenage girls were sexually active; the figure is almost 50 percent today. During the same time period, the sexual-activity rate for teenage boys more than doubled, from an estimated 25 percent to over 50 percent. By the time they leave high school, some 90 percent of seniors are no longer virgins. And, while close to 70 percent of teenagers use some form of contraception, most use it ineffectively. There are more than 1 million teenage pregnancies in this country each year — a higher percentage than in any other Western country, even those where the sexual activity rates for teenagers are comparable to our own. In addition, sexually transmitted diseases among teenagers have reached epidemic proportions.

The Second Sexual Revolution

This increased sexual activity of teenagers is primarily the result of the "second sexual revolution." The first sexual revolution occurred in the last century, when — for the first time — individuals began to choose mates on the basis of mutual attraction, rather than on the basis of parental or community authority. The second sexual revolution occurred during the 1960's, when pre-marital sex became socially acceptable in this country.

Adolescents routinely imitate adult behavior. When adults demonstrated abstinence until after marriage, teenagers were encouraged to do the same. Now that pre-marital sex is common among adults and vividly portrayed in all of the media, teenagers have followed this new adult example.

Despite the second sexual revolution and its excesses, a large proportion of teenagers today are not sexually active, and do not become pregnant or contract venereal disease. The real question we have to ask, then, is why some people in general — and some teens in particular — are prone to take such risks. Is it that they do not know any better? In that case, sex education at home and in the schools would be a meaningful solution.

Most young people who are sexually active, however, are well aware of the dangers of pregnancy and of venereal disease. Obviously, education in and of itself does not control behavior. Most people are well aware of the dangers of smoking, for example, and yet many, many people continue to smoke.

One key to explaining why people take risks may lie in what I call the *personal fable*. This is a belief that bad things will happen to other people, but not to us. The personal fable can serve a useful function by taking some of the fear out of potentially dangerous situations like flying in airplanes.

In terms of teenage sex, however, the fable is less than helpful. A belief in our personal invulnerability makes its first appearance in adolescence, and is particularly strong in those teenagers who feel insecure, unwanted, and unloved. Such teenagers have a great need to feel special in some way. When the social prohibitions are down, when the media supports casual sex, and when peer-group pressures are strong, these teens feel coerced into engaging in sexual activity at an early age. And, the fable tells them that doing so is okay, because nothing bad will happen to them.

What Parents Can Do

Although we cannot control the pressures on our children that come from outside the family, we do have a measure of control over what goes on within our homes. We can, from an early age, set limits and standards that our children can use to internalize their own limits and standards.

In addition, as suggested previously, frequent and open discussions about sexual activity are a necessity in today's world. Although such discussions are difficult and uncomfortable, they are very important. We have to remember that the difficulty and discomfort we deal with in discussing sexual matters is far less than the difficulty and discomfort we will experience if our teenager becomes pregnant or contracts a venereal disease.

Contrary to popular opinion, most young people engage in sexual activity for psychological rather than hormonal reasons. If teenagers feel secure, loved, and appreciated at home, they are not likely to seek comfort and support elsewhere in the form of premature sexual intimacy.

PREVENTING DATE RAPE

Estelle (not her real name) spoke in a low voice, just a decibel or two above a whisper, and the words came out slowly. Her story was a sadly familiar one. She told me that she was not a very popular girl, and that when J. asked her out for the second time, she was "wicked happy." She really liked him and began to let herself hope that he liked her, too. On the second date, after seeing a movie, J. drove to a deserted beach. Estelle thought they would look at the stars, listen to the waves, and talk. But, J. started to kiss her and touch her all over. Estelle kept blaming herself for not saying no sooner, but she wanted him to like her and had no idea that he would force himself on her. I had to repeat her own words to her: "But, you did say no, and you did tell him you didn't want to do that, didn't you?" She replied, "Yes, I did. Why did he do it?"

Estelle, like so many victims of date rape, was experiencing the pain of many different — often conflicting — emotions and depressive feelings. There was guilt about having had intercourse, combined with hate and loathing for both the boy and for herself. But, stronger than all the rest was a wrenching, overwhelming sense of shame — that everyone knew and that everyone had passed judgment on her. It was only after Estelle participated in therapy that she was able to accept herself again and really believe it wasn't her fault.

Date rape appears to be on the increase, particularly among teenagers. It is estimated that 1 in 5 young women nationwide will be raped on a date, but only about 5 percent will report it. The most frequent victims are ages 15 to 24. In terms of definition, as soon as the victim says no and then sexual touching or other sexual activity occurs, it is rape or some form of sexual assault. This type of attack may be committed primarily out of anger, or a need to feel powerful and dominate another person. While a young man may try to rationalize his actions as a result of his being carried away by strong sexual drives, there is no excuse for this behavior.

Contemporary Dating Patterns

Among today's teenagers, it is now considered socially acceptable — indeed, often desirable — to engage in sex prior to marriage. The only question that remains is not "if" but "when." Both boys and girls know this, and it has transformed the psychological atmosphere of dating.

Current social practices are also contributing to this new atmosphere. Boys and girls used to go out in groups. For many contemporary teenagers, however, "going out" is a modern version of "going steady." And, when asked if three months was a long enough time to go together before expecting intercourse, a group of New England high school students chorused, "Oh, yeeeaaahhh."

This new social climate has the effect of making young men more assertive in their sexual demands, and young women less forceful in their resistance. Many teenage date-rape victims believe that if they have said "no" and the boy persists, they have no choice but to give in. Yet, girls do have a choice, and there are things we can do to help them avoid — or at least minimize — the possibility of date rape.

What Parents Can Do

One of the things we can teach our daughters is to express themselves more forcibly, so that their words convey the true strength of their opposition. This amounts to a kind of assertiveness training. We should also insist that our daughters initially engage in common-sense practices such as double dating and going out only with groups, as safeguards against sexual assault. We also need to caution our daughters that alcohol and drugs can impair their judgment and make them more vulnerable to date rape.

Eventually, however, a young woman will want to go out on single dates. On such occasions, it is important for her to find out in advance exactly where she and her date will be going, what stops they will be making, and at what time they will return. Whenever possible, she should also obtain the relevant phone numbers. She should give us this information and tell her date that she has done so. She can explain that we routinely request this information in case of an emergency. In this way, the young man is informed in an inoffensive way that we are monitoring the date. While this practice will not absolutely prevent date rape, it will help to discourage it.

Obviously, some date rapes cannot be avoided. And, in advocating measures that we parents can take to help our daughters avoid such assaults, I am *not* suggesting that they are responsible or in any way inviting rape. We must also teach our sons that date rape is not only morally wrong — it is also a punishable crime.

SEXUALLY TRANSMITTED DISEASES

"I can't believe it. My girlfriend told me she was a virgin, but she gave me gonorrhea. When I told her, she claimed she must have been infected by a toilet seat. I asked my doctor, and he said she couldn't have gotten it that way. What a bummer; she lied to me about being a virgin, and now she is lying about how she caught it. Live and learn, I guess."

This 17-year-old is one of a growing number of teenagers infected with a sexually transmitted disease (STD). The potential effects of such infection include pelvic inflammatory disease and associated chronic pelvic pain, as well as tubal infertility in young women. For both male and female teenagers, STD infection is also associated with vulnerability to genital cancers and to infection by the AIDS virus.

Although there was a decline in the rates of gonorrhea infection during the 1980's (as a result of a major campaign against this disease), there is every indication that the overall rates of STD infection among teenagers continue to increase, particularly among younger adolescents. This growing incidence of STD's is directly attributable to the increase in teenage sexual activity, which — as I pointed out in an earlier piece — grew out of the "second sexual revolution" and the social acceptability of premarital intercourse.

The earlier a teenager becomes sexually active, the longer the period of exposure to different sex partners. And, the more partners a teenager has, the greater the risk of contracting an STD. The interval between 15 and 19 years of age now appears to be the highest risk period for exposure to multiple sex partners and, therefore, to STD's.

A Major Epidemic

As a result, some 3 million teenagers contract an STD each year. Although teenagers are most concerned about contracting AIDS, only about 1 percent of all reported AIDS cases occur among adolescents. Yet, 1 in 4 sexually active teenagers will contract an STD before leaving high school. Teenagers should be aware that they may contract chlamydia (the most common form of bacterial STD), genital warts, herpes, gonorrhea, or syphilis, and that these diseases may have serious consequences, including increased vulnerability to AIDS infection.

Unfortunately, many teenagers have erroneous ideas about preventing venereal disease. And, even when they have been given accurate information, many teens continue to deny their vulnerability to sexually transmitted diseases and to pregnancy. Recent surveys found that between 38 and 66 percent of teenagers reported using condoms during their last coital episode. In general, it appears that most teenagers use condoms irregularly.

Most experts agree that sex education in our schools has not been effective in encouraging either abstinence or the use of contraceptives. Often, sex education courses are taught after many teenagers have already become sexually active. In addition, too many of these programs focus on the biology rather than the psychology of sexual interaction. Nonetheless, there is one kind of sexual education that does make an impact. If a teenager who has contracted a venereal disease, or who has become pregnant, shares the experience with other teenagers, the effect is powerful. Such presentations are the most effective means of destroying a teenager's belief that "it can't possibly happen to me."

What Parents Can Do

As I have suggested throughout this chapter, we may feel uncomfortable discussing sex with our teenagers, but it is critical that we talk about STD's and the possible consequences mentioned above (infertility and cancer, among others). We may choose to counsel our adolescent to postpone becoming sexually active, but we should also make it clear that whenever he or she becomes sexually active, condom use should be as habitual as using a seat belt in a car. These days especially, we must do all we can to ensure that our teenager does not contract an STD.

TEENS' SEXUAL PRIVACY VERSUS PARENTS' RIGHT TO KNOW

During adolescence, young people become much more private about their lives. The increased desire for privacy begins around puberty, when new intellectual abilities emerge which allow teens to appreciate for the first time that no one else knows what they are thinking. They realize that they can engage in socially unacceptable thoughts and fantasies with impunity. And, because the teenager's world is new and fragile, he or she is very concerned about maintaining that privacy for *all* thoughts, particularly the sexual ones.

As much as possible, we should respect teenagers' privacy in general and their sexual privacy in particular. It is best not to try to probe their thoughts and feelings.

Difficult Decisions

There are, however, times when a teenager's wish for sexual privacy is more serious and complex. If, for example, a young person learns that he or she has a venereal disease, the physician may be asked not to tell the parents. Some teenagers ask this out of a sincere desire to protect their parents from unhappiness. Other teens' motives are quite different: these adolescents are afraid of what might happen to them if their parents find out. Some realistically fear that they will be verbally or physically abused. Because these young people believe that they cannot share their lives with their parents, they may feel guilty, angry at their parents and themselves, and generally depressed. Professional help may well be appropriate in such cases.

Most health professionals' policy is to share with parents only information that the teenager wishes to be shared. From a professional point of view, regardless of the nature of the condition, the health professional is ethically bound to honor the young person's desire for privacy. The only exception is when the teen's life might be in danger. Still, problems may arise when the teenager's right to privacy conflicts with the parents' right to be informed — for example, if the teenager has a venereal disease, is pregnant, or wants an abortion.

How to proceed in this sort of situation is not clear from a legal point of view. It has been argued that teenagers have the same constitutional right to privacy guaranteed to adults in our society. On the other hand, it has also been argued that since teenagers under 18 are minors under the law, they should have parental permission before they are treated for a disease or can obtain an abortion. These issues are now being fought out in the courts.

What Parents Can Do

Open communication between parents and children is a relatively modern phenomenon, and a very healthy one. If teenagers have a history of comfortable communication with their parents, they will be willing to share even unpleasant information with them, and will expect to receive reassurance and guidance. It is also true that teenagers who have such a relationship with their parents are the least likely to have unhappy news to share. Teenagers who have little or no history of open communication with their parents feel the strongest need to guard their sexual privacy, and it is they who must often demand that health professionals do the same.

SEXUALLY ACTIVE TEENS

"Should I give my 16-year-old son condoms?" a woman in the audience asked me after a lecture. "He is going to be a camp counselor for two months, and I know that he is sexually active. I don't want to encourage him, but I know he will be active whether I encourage him or not, and I'm afraid of the risks of his not using protection."

As a well-trained psychologist (who knows that if you don't have an answer to a question, you can always ask another one), I inquired, "Can you and your son talk comfortably about his being sexually active?" To which the mother replied, "Yes, we have talked about the responsibilities that go along with sexual freedom." I then said, "Under those circumstances, it does make sense to provide him with condoms."

A quarter of a century ago, I would have answered this question in the negative. Different times, however, call for different measures. It would be foolish to deny contemporary reality and the second sexual revolution, now that almost 50 percent of teenagers are sexually active by age 15, and 90 percent are no longer virgins by the time they leave high school. However much we might wish we could return to that earlier, less liberal era, such a return is impossible. Like it or not, we have to deal with the reality of sexually active teens.

What Parents Can Do

Throughout their childhoods, we have taught our children the contractual rule that every freedom they enjoy — from riding their bikes to spending the night at a friend's house — is dependent upon their acting responsibly. If they are not responsible, they will necessarily experience a corresponding loss of freedom. The same holds true for sexual behavior.

What we must get across to teenagers is that if they are going to enjoy the freedom of being sexually active, then they must also be sexually responsible. In this day and age, sexual responsibility entails taking measures not only to prevent pregnancy, but also to protect oneself from being exposed to HIV (the virus that leads to AIDS) and from contracting other sexually transmitted diseases.

The mother who asked me the question with which this piece began was deeply worried that her son might contract some sexually transmitted disease, or that he might get a girl pregnant. By providing her son with condoms, she was reinforcing the freedom-responsibility contract.

As I mentioned previously, we may also want to counsel our teenager to postpone sexual activity until a later age. Many teens choose this route for practical reasons, such as concerns about infection and unwanted pregnancies. Others abstain for moral or personal reasons. We parents need to tell our sons and daughters that saying "I don't want to engage in that activity" is a responsible and acceptable option. We can support our teenager in exercising this option by helping them find the words to explain their choice to their peers.

As parents, we may agonize over the fact that our teenager is sexually active, and hope that he or she chooses to abstain. But, if the young person doesn't, the only practical thing we can do — in a spirit of love and concern — is to encourage the use of condoms.

3
FAMILY MATTERS

OVERVIEW

Adolescence is a time when young people want desperately to have the prerogatives of adulthood, yet hate to give up the equally attractive prerogatives of childhood. Not surprisingly, teenagers constantly vacillate between strivings for independence from the family and regressions to childish dependence on it.

As noted earlier, this is also a time when many of us parents are confronting our own conflicts regarding stability and change. At mid-life, we may be trying to decide whether or not to make changes in our career, whether or not to move to a different locale, and perhaps even whether or not to stay with our mate. Many symptoms of teenage ambivalence, such as rudeness or avoiding family outings, are all the more aggravating when we are dealing with our own ambivalent feelings. While it is difficult at such times to be as objective and caring as we might otherwise be, we must make the effort to deal with our teenagers and related family matters on their own terms, rather than letting them become an outlet for our own inner conflicts.

Of course, one reason this approach can be difficult is that we may often be uncertain what our teenagers are thinking and feeling. The first section of this chapter contains a set of questions which can help us check our understanding of a teenager, by trying to predict his or her behavior in certain situations. If we also let our teenager do the same with us, this questionnaire can be a useful starting point for family discussions.

In our effort to understand our teenagers, we must recognize that an adolescent's efforts to grow up sometimes appear to be a rejection of the family. This is certainly the case when our teenager refuses to go along on traditional family outings. If we view this as an attempt to establish independence — and not as a personal rejection — we are better prepared to explore different options that can lead to a mutually satisfactory compromise. In a similar way, a teenager can also affront us with his or her choice of clothing, but if we recognize these choices as experiments with identity, we can be more accepting and work out an agreement that meets everyone's needs.

Perhaps the most difficult teenage behavior to handle is outright rudeness. While we should not acquiesce to such rudeness, we also should not attack it as evidence of bad character. Instead, we need to recognize it as another expression of teenagers' ambivalence about growing up, and express our anger without attacking or lecturing the adolescent. We need to behave in a similar way when the teenager fails to do what he or she has agreed to do. Rather than complain and demand, we can focus on how and when the task will be done. And, we need to be able to provide constructive criticism, offering sympathetic guidance and instruction which is responsible and does not attack the teenager.

Setting limits is another aspect of parenting that can be troublesome when adolescents are struggling with issues of dependence and independence. Reasonable limits are important and should be set in advance, so that everyone involved has a clear understanding of the consequences of serious violations. At the same time, we have to be careful about prohibiting what we cannot prevent, and we have to follow through with the promised consequences when necessary. Related issues arise when teenagers engage us in power struggles, in order to assert their independence and to develop their own morals and values. In response, we need to be clear and firm in our beliefs, providing adolescents with a foil against which they can test their self-constructed ethics.

Privacy issues can present particularly difficult ethical dilemmas within the family. In general, young people should be entitled to the same privacy that we extend to our spouses and our friends. Privacy, however, is a freedom that is dependent upon the teenager's demonstration of responsibility. If the teenager is irresponsible and abuses privacy to conceal something like drug abuse, then he or she forfeits the freedom from intrusion.

Probably the most difficult family issue for teenagers is a divorce. Even though divorce is more common today than it was in the past, it is no less painful and disorienting for adolescents. We help most when we inform teenagers about the decision as soon as possible, reassure them about what will happen to them, and restate our abiding love for them. After a divorce, we serve teenagers best by minimizing the amount of change and stress they experience, and not trying to use them to punish a former spouse.

Grandparents can be a blessing for teenagers when there are serious family problems, and when there are not. Often, our parents can be more objective and accepting of our children than we can. But, sometimes the relationships that develop between grandparents and teenagers can create problems within the family. At such times, we need to follow the general principles of sound parenting — fairness, firmness, and love — in dealing with these matters.

One of the most challenging aspects of the parenting process — letting our children become independent adults — is also our most important goal in regard to adolescents' struggles to achieve their own identity. Although we never cease being parents, once our children are grown we can enter into a new, more mutual relationship. At that point, we are likely to find that our adult children value our company and counsel more than they did when they were teenagers.

Achieving this goal requires us to appreciate each teenager as a unique individual going through the normal stresses and strains of growth. We do this best by recognizing that many of the trials and tribulations our teenager puts us through are in the service of self-definition and self-discovery. When we regard confrontations within the family this way, they lose their sting of rejection and ungratefulness.

While helping a teenager become an independent, responsible adult, we must also let the young person know that we are still available to provide support and guidance. The best evidence we have that our teenager has attained the appropriate balance between independence and dependence is when he or she freely chooses to come to us for counsel, but then makes a decision independently. At such times, we should be both happy and proud that our teen is secure enough to ask for needed help, and mature enough to use it wisely.

HOW WELL DO YOU KNOW YOUR TEEN?

Perhaps the best test of whether or not we really know someone else is our ability to predict his or her behavior. Not just any behavior, however. When my sons were young, I could predict with almost 100% accuracy what they were going to order at McDonald's. That ability came mostly from having observed them in the same situation many times before. A better test of whether or not we can predict another person's behavior is our ability to predict how he or she will respond to a novel situation.

To help you determine how well you know your teenager, I have described a few novel situations and provided an assortment of predictions as to how your teenager would react. After choosing the predictions you think are most likely, have your teenager take the test. Then, compare your predictions. A 60% accuracy rate is about the average for parents. If you do much better than that, you get the "Freud Award." If you do less well, spend more time talking with your teen.

Do-You-Know-Your-Teenager Test

● *The family cat has knocked over the garbage pail and made a mess on the kitchen floor. Your teenager is the first person to see the mess. Your teenager:*
   (a) cleans it up,
   (b) cleans some of it,
   (c) steps over the mess on the way to his or her room.

● *Your teenager has been preparing for an important competition but is forced to withdraw because of illness. Your teenager:*

(a) takes it philosophically,

(b) is upset but gets over it reasonably quickly,

(c) stays angry and depressed for weeks.

● *Your teenager has enough money to buy his or her sibling an attractive gift that the sibling would really enjoy. Your teenager:*

(a) buys the gift with pleasure,

(b) buys the gift with reservations,

(c) buys a less expensive gift.

● *Your teenager has asked you to buy him or her an expensive piece of designer clothing that many peers are wearing. You say no. Your teenager:*

(a) accepts your decision without resentment,

(b) accepts the decision but resents it,

(c) does not accept the decision and quarrels about it.

● *Your teenager says that he or she has finished the day's homework and should be allowed to go out. Your teenager:*

(a) is telling the truth,

(b) has stretched the truth a little bit,

(c) has stretched the truth a lot.

● *The school provides opportunities for young people to do volunteer work with the aged. Your teenager:*

(a) volunteers,

(b) would like to but has too many other obligations,

(c) won't volunteer.

● *Your teenager has the opportunity to be sexually active with another teenager to whom he or she is attracted. Your teenager:*

(a) talks to you about it and asks your advice,

(b) refers to the matter in an indirect and guarded manner

(c) refuses to discuss it with you altogether.

● *In your absence, someone puts you down verbally in front of your son or daughter. Your teenager:*

(a) defends you vigorously, regardless of the criticism,

(b) is upset but says nothing,

(c) would not hesitate to agree with the critic.

● *When taking a test, your teenager observes another student cheating. Your teenager:*

(a) talks to the other student about it,

(b) does nothing,

(c) goes directly to the authorities.

What Parents Can Do

I offer this test as a means of encouraging reflection and discussion between you and your teenager. And, since "turn-about is fair play," you might let your teenager predict how you would have reacted to these situations when you were a teenager!

PARENTAL INVOLVEMENT

Hebrew school always bored me. I found it frustrating to be learning to read words that I didn't understand. The teacher was a former tailor, Mr. Rabinovitch. We never got along, and one day he yelled at me for drawing horses instead of paying attention. I ran out into the winter night without my coat while the astounded Mr. Rabinovitch rumbled after me. I ran into an alley and — remembering a cartoon I had seen — climbed into a trash can and pulled the lid over me.

As soon as I was sure the coast was clear, I climbed out of the trash can and ran home. When my mother saw me, coatless and smelling of garbage, she became very angry. With me in tow, now in a jacket, we tramped back through the snow to the school. As we entered the classroom, my mother let loose with a nicely prioritized list of Yiddish curses that were new to me: "Break both of your legs and then go dancing" was among the most choice. That was the end of my Hebrew school career.

I recite this episode because it illustrates the fact that as parents we tend to become involved in our teenager's schooling or work when something either goes very wrong or very right. To be sure, we may make the routine visit to school on parents' night, or the ritual outing to our teen's place of work, but that is about it. And, by and large most adolescents prefer it that way.

What Parents Can Do

There are times, however, when it is necessary for us to become more actively involved with our teenager's school or place of work. When, for example, a young person's grades go down, or he or she is physically or sexually harassed at school, we need to talk to the teachers, school counselor, or principal. While the teenager may resist our interventions on such occasions, it is important that we take action. And, despite his or her proclaimed unhappiness at our involvement, a teenager takes at least some satisfaction in knowing that we care enough to find out what is going on and attempt to correct the situation.

The same holds true for our involvement at an adolescent's place of work. Generally, we have more latitude here, since the teenager is free to quit a job which results in mistreatment. Nonetheless, there are times when intervention is appropriate. An example would be a teenage girl who is being asked to work excessively long shifts and does so out of loyalty to the employer. If this happens, we have to make it clear to the teen that the long hours are detrimental to her health and school work. We have to say that if she will not ask for shorter hours, then she will have to quit the job. In this sort of situation, it is best to put the responsibility on the teenager, so that she can have the valuable experience of standing up for herself.

Whether or not to intervene in a young person's life is a difficult decision. Even when we are asked to help, we still have to question whether it is healthy for us to do so, or whether it is better for the teenager to handle it with our support.

It's useful to ask ourselves first, "What action can I take, or refrain from taking, that will do the most to foster my child's sense of independence and feelings of competence?" Secondly, it is important not to expect — nor to demand — that our teenagers handle situations better than we might ourselves. Some of us are still reluctant to speak up to an employer, even when we have a legitimate grievance. And, that is okay. We are all human, and no one is fully grown-up at any age.

Growing up is difficult, and letting go is no easier. We will never make all the right decisions about when — and when not — to intrude into our adolescent's affairs. The important thing is that we care enough to make the effort to distance ourselves from our personal issues, and to intervene only when it is in the best interests of our child.

WHEN TEENS BOYCOTT FAMILY OUTINGS

"We've been going on the same dumb family camping trip over Fourth of July weekend since I was 2-years-old," a teenager recently confided in me. "I really don't want to go this year. I want to hang out with my friends. But, my parents are making me go."

There comes a time in almost every family when a teenager no longer wants to go on outings with his or her parents. The teen may consider participation in such events childish, or may feel that spending time with friends is more fun. Whatever the reason, the message from the teenager to the parents is very clear: "Being with you guys is boring!"

When your teenager tells you that he or she would rather be with friends than with you, it is natural to feel upset and angry. Family traditions, such as annual outings, are important because they provide a sense of togetherness and continuity with the past, as well as happy anticipation of the future. A teenager's reluctance to go on outings may therefore feel like a rejection of the family and its traditions. In fact, however, it is more likely to be an expression of growing independence and should be taken seriously.

What Parents Can Do

At the same time, our feelings as parents are important, too. We need to explain to our teenagers that although we understand their needs, we also miss having them along with us.

In addition, there are several options and compromises we can explore when a teenager reaches this stage of development. For example, I suggested to the young man mentioned earlier that he ask his parents whether he might take one of his friends along on the camping trip. His parents agreed, and in this case, the arrangement proved to be a happy solution for everyone concerned.

We can also encourage our teens to become more involved in planning family outings. Even when the outing is a traditional or required one, such as a visit to a relative's home, there are always choices as to which route to take, and where to eat and stay along the way. Asking teenagers about their preferences may make them more inclined to participate. Although the final say is ours, we need to listen and — when possible — act on the suggestions. We also have to recognize that adolescents "need their own space," which we can provide by allowing them to do things on their own once we arrive at our destination.

We can also allow a teenager to skip a family outing occasionally. Some young people are quite trustworthy and can take care of themselves for a day or two without any problems. Others, however, are less mature and responsible, so it is important that we make arrangements for these teenagers to stay with relatives or a friend's family.

The good news for us parents is that a young person's reluctance to spend time with the family will not last forever.

When my own sons were teenagers, they groaned at the mere mention of a family outing. Now that they are young adults, they frequently initiate these gatherings themselves. If we recognize that a teenager's rejection of family outings is a necessary stage of growing up — and not an attack on us as parents — we can accept it more easily and look forward to a time when the family can once again join forces.

CLASHES OVER CLOTHES

Children dress to please their parents, young adolescents dress to please their peers, and older teenagers dress to please themselves. This may be somewhat of an over-simplification, but it does highlight the most common motivations behind young people's style of dress at successive stages of development.

During late adolescence, teenagers are struggling to form a sense of identity — a sense of who they are that is consistent with what they have achieved in the past and what they hope to become in the future. Experimentation with clothing is often part of this search for identity.

For example, one young woman I know chose a bohemian look during her junior year of high school, wearing vivid makeup and loose, peasant-like clothing. The next year, she adopted a conservative style with subtle makeup and tailored clothing. During her first year of college, she finally found a fashionable, middle-of-the-road style that was truly her own.

Changes of this sort do not signal insecurity or indecisiveness; they are simply the outward reflection of experimentation with several different identities. Punk styles or ponytails for boys, to cite two other examples, are simply the most recent and flamboyant manifestations of this age-old process.

Just as teenagers need to be free to experiment with other facets of their identities, they need to be free to experiment with clothing. But, freedom has its limits. When young people want to purchase and wear truly outlandish or sexually provocative clothing, disagreements may arise.

What Parents Can Do

When dealing with my adolescent sons, I discovered that there was no way we could agree on what was outlandish or provocative. At first, I tried a heavy-handed, "thou-shalt-not" approach, which didn't really work. Then, by luck, I discovered mediation. Bernie, a good friend whom my sons admired, was visiting when one of the boys was wearing jeans which I thought were too tight. My son and I decided to let Bernie be the judge, agreeing to abide by his decision.

To my dismay and annoyance, Bernie didn't think the jeans were that bad. But, from that day on, my sons and I always tried to bring in a neutral third party (such as an older sibling or a sales clerk) whenever we had a difference of opinion over which clothes to buy or wear. This approach meant that each of us prevailed sometimes. It also taught me that my concern over my sons' dress arose, at least in part, from how their appearance reflected on me as a parent. If I was honest, I had to admit that I was more concerned about what their dress said about me than what it said about them.

My sons and I also hit upon another compromise that allowed them to wear clothing which I regarded as outlandish when they were with their friends, but to keep my feelings in mind when we were in public together. One son, frequently given to wearing the same loud polyester shirt and baggy pants, agreed to dress "boring" when we went out, as long as he could make his own fashion statement when he was with his friends.

Eventually, I learned — as all parents of adolescents must — to suffer teenage dress at least with tolerance, if not gladly. Such experimentation is only a passing phase. Most adolescents find a clothing style that is in keeping with the personality of the young person whom we have always known and loved.

"MY TEEN IS SO RUDE!"

"Justin, would you take out the trash?"
"You do it. You're closer."

Or, "Clarissa, have you finished your homework?"
"Stop bugging me. It's my homework, not yours."

These are just two examples of typical teenage remarks likely to make us parents apoplectic. Although the news may be small comfort, most kids are rude and defiant at one time or another during their teen years. Girls will usually engage parents (particularly their mother) in verbal battles. Boys are more likely to express themselves by physical acts, such as slamming the door when they leave the house. Both types of behavior are a challenge to our authority, but also a bid for an emotional response.

In most cases, teenagers' rudeness is an expression of their ambivalence about their growing independence. While they yearn to be grown-up and mature, at times they also long to be children again. It's when young people feel this pull to childhood most acutely that they are most likely to be rude.

In a teenager's mind, defiance expresses autonomy and says that he or she doesn't need us. This behavior also serves another purpose, however. By infuriating us and drawing us into a confrontation, an adolescent receives reassurance that we still care. Ironically, our anger and exasperation are taken as an expression of our continuing love and commitment.

What Parents Can Do

It's okay to grow angry at a teenager's rudeness, but we should express our anger immediately and briefly. This is much more effective than swallowing our anger and later lecturing our teenager about the evils of his or her ways, as well as the dire future in store if such behavior continues. Lectures, unfortunately, tend to focus on the young person's character and may include statements such as, "You never think about anyone but yourself." In contrast, when we express our feelings immediately, we can talk about those feelings rather than our teenager's character, using statements such as "It really makes me furious when you talk to me that way."

It is also important to let our teenager know that rudeness will not keep us from fulfilling our commitments and responsibilities as parents. For example, if the teen talks back to us when we ask him or her to do some basic chore, we might respond by saying, "Look, I'll drive you to the mall and give you money for clothes as I promised. But, I want you to know that I still expect you to do your chores, and I don't care for your rudeness."

While some parents might argue that this will only encourage teenage rudeness, I do not believe this to be the case. In fact, if we respond to rudeness by verbally attacking an adolescent and breaking our commitments, the teenager will feel that the rudeness was justified. If, instead, we refrain from retaliating and do fulfill the bargains that we have made, the teen can only feel a bit embarrassed and ashamed about the rude behavior.

When we handle teenage rudeness this way, we provide a positive example of adult responsibility. It also lets the teenager know that we can cope with his or her growing pains without regressing to a primitive "eye for an eye, tooth for a tooth" morality.

NAG, NAG, NAG

I don't like avocados. When I was growing up in California, we had an avocado tree in our backyard, and my job was to pick the ripe avocados and transport them to salad-loving friends, neighbors, and relatives. To this day, I can still hear my mother saying, "Did you pick the avocados yet?" All I learned from being nagged about avocados was to hate them in any form.

When we nag teenagers, we annoy them by persistent fault-finding, complaints, or demands. This parental behavior tends to occur when our children neglect some duty that is routinely expected of them, such as cleaning their room, doing their homework, taking out the garbage, or — in my case — picking avocados. The fact is that nagging is more often an expression of our own frustration than an effective teaching tool.

That's where the problem lies: when nagging doesn't work, we become more frustrated and, in turn, step up the nagging. This makes it even more ineffective and creates a vicious cycle, with flaring tempers and bitter words usually the result.

Young people fail to carry out routine activities for any number of reasons. Forgetting what needs to be done, however, is usually not one of them. Yet, such forgetting is just what nagging pre-supposes. In most cases, the reasons lie elsewhere. Some teenagers neglect their chores as a way of asserting their new autonomy and independence. Other teens simply find the activities rather burdensome and boring. And, many times adolescents simply cannot understand why their parents seem so fixated on a particular activity, such as cleaning their bedrooms, especially when the teens themselves are genuinely not bothered by clothes, books, and papers scattered all over the floor.

What Parents Can Do

An effective alternate to nagging is to speak to the particular job that needs to be done, rather than to the teenager's personal deficiencies. In their book *How To Talk So Kids Will Listen & Listen So Kids Will Talk*, Adele Faber and Elaine Mazlish offer the following approach:

Father: Steve, it's been two weeks since the lawn was mowed. I'd like it done today.
Son: Sure, Dad. Later.
Father: I'd feel better if I knew just when you plan to get to it.
Son: As soon as this program is over.
Father: When is that?
Son: In about an hour.
Father: Good. Now I know I can count on the lawn being done one hour from now. Thanks, Steve.

When it comes to your teen's sloppy bedroom, the best tactic may simply be to accept the mess and close the door. The message is, "Your room is your room, and if you can live in that mess, it's your business. But, the rest of the house belongs to everyone, and in those rooms, we expect you to pick up after yourself."

Or, if the messy room really gets to you, you can try making the following offer: "Look, I will help you clean up your room, if you will help me clean up mine." A teenager is much more likely to respond positively to this offer of cooperative effort than to an ultimatum.

Getting an adolescent to do what he or she should do or needs to do is not always easy. But, our natural reaction — nagging — is not productive and, in fact, often makes the situation worse. An important rule for parents is to focus on what needs to be done, when it will be done, and how it will be done. By centering our attention on the goal to be accomplished, rather than on our teenager's character or personality, we are more likely to attain the desired result.

HOW TO CRITICIZE
SO TEENS WILL LISTEN

A number of years ago, psychologist Haim G. Ginott wrote the following about parents' criticism of teenagers:

"Most parental criticism is unhelpful. It creates anger, resentment, and a desire for revenge. When a teenager is constantly criticized he learns to condemn himself and to find fault with others. He learns to doubt his own worth, and to belittle the value of others. He learns to suspect people and to expect personal doom. Most criticism is unnecessary. When we take a wrong turn on a road and lose our way, the last thing we need is criticism. It is not helpful to have our driving skills analyzed and evaluated at this point. What we need is a friendly person to give us clear directions."

Although we might all agree with Ginott in theory, I, for one, have sometimes found it difficult to put his very sound ideas into practice. For example, when my son neglected to let our dog out and the animal had an "accident" on our new living room rug, I was hard pressed to be a "friendly person" who offered "directions." Instead, I wanted to lash out and tell my son how irresponsible he had been, even though I knew the negative effect that criticism has on young people. My emotions were simply too strong for me to follow Ginott's advice.

What Parents Can Do

Fortunately, there is an effective, non-punitive way for us to express our anger and frustration. We can share our indignation with our teen through a humorous exaggeration of our feelings, rather than through a scathing description of his character and personality. For example, you might say, "If you forget to take out the trash one more time, I'm going to send you to the moon." Or, "The next time you come in after curfew, I'll ground you for so long that you'll think you're Rip Van Winkle by the time you see daylight again." In the case of my son, I might have said something to the effect of, "If that dog has another accident in the house, you'll be washing dishes from here to eternity."

These sorts of statements are helpful because they allow us to express our feelings in non-hurtful ways. By using exaggerated expressions of our anger, we can let off steam without attacking an adolescent's self-esteem. This is easy to understand when we compare the above remarks with comments such as, "You are so irresponsible" or "You are so thoughtless."

Exaggerated statements also help us get our emotions under control. And, once our emotions are in check, it is much easier to be that friendly person who gives directions (or in my case, who helped his son clean up after the dog).

There is, of course, a place for constructive criticism, which is also much easier to engage in when our emotions are under control. Constructive criticism is effective because it grows out of respect and caring for others, rather than out of anger and a desire for revenge. When a teenager, for example, inadvertently says something that is hurtful to a friend, it is appropriate to tell the teen something like, "Look, we all say things we don't really mean sometimes. I am sure you didn't mean what you said to Nicky, and I know that he would like to hear that from you."

Unlike negative criticism, which attacks an adolescent's sense of self and has no redeeming value, constructive criticism allows us to challenge the young person's behavior and still deliver a positive message. There is also a fringe benefit to criticizing in a positive way: by criticizing without rancor, we provide a model teenagers can follow when they need to criticize someone else's behavior.

SETTING LIMITS

"Okay, now that you are 14, you can use lip gloss, but you will have to pay for it out of your own babysitting money," a mother told her daughter. She then added with great emphasis, "But, no eye makeup!"

Effective limit setting is as much a matter of attitude as it is of specific rules or prohibitions. This mother — by her voice and demeanor — made it very clear that she felt strongly about her daughter wearing eye makeup, and that she was prepared to back up that concern with action. When discussing limits with your teenager, communicating the strength of your feelings in a similar way is important, because it lets your teen know that you mean business.

In the best of all possible worlds, we should begin setting limits when our children are young, as this helps them prepare to set their own limits when they reach adolescence. Unfortunately, many of us learn this priceless bit of wisdom only after our children are half grown.

Teenagers' resistance to our limit setting is often set off not so much by the limits as by the timing: "You let me choose my friends when I was small. You let me eat junk food when I was a kid. You didn't worry about my clothes when I was in second grade. Why are you coming down on me now?" These are common but often unvoiced complaints of teenagers. Many adolescents feel that they were allowed — indeed, encouraged — to take charge of their lives when they were children, only to be told that they are no longer in charge now that they are teenagers. Not surprisingly, this makes them angry and rebellious.

What Parents Can Do

In such situations, honesty is often the best policy. We can say to our teen, "Look, I know that I should have been stricter when you were younger, and I know you feel that I set you up to expect freedom but now I am taking it away from you. I will also be honest and say that I am setting limits now as much for myself as for you. I really do worry about you, and I am setting limits because I love you."

One basic rule in setting limits is not to lay down any prohibitions that you cannot enforce. You can *forbid* your teenager to smoke (cigarettes or marijuana), but you cannot *prevent* the teen from doing so because you are not with him or her all of the time. An alternative is to come right out and say, "I know that I cannot prevent you from smoking, but if I find out that you have been smoking, you will be grounded for a week with no allowance." When you make your position very clear in advance of any violation of the limits, your teenager cannot argue that he or she did not know the rules.

Curfews are perhaps the most common limit set by parents. Midnight — or, at most, one o'clock — on weekends is a reasonable curfew. Teenagers may challenge this limit, but many come to appreciate it. The father of a 16-year-old girl told me that initially his daughter fought him on his midnight curfew. Then, one Saturday night she came home at the designated time with a smile on her face. "You are looking very happy," he commented. She replied, "Yeah, some creeps crashed the party, and I was the only one who had a good reason to leave!"

Although adolescents may resist our limits, on a deeper level they also know that our setting limits shows we are concerned enough to take the risk of confrontation and rebellion. As one teenager said about a friend who had free access to his parents' liquor cabinet, "I guess Jack's parents don't love him, or they wouldn't let him do that, would they?" With this question, the young man verbalized the idea that a lack of reasonable limits may be equated with a lack of love and concern.

By setting limits and following through with promised consequences when necessary, we show our teenagers that despite their adult size and increasing independence, we understand that they are not fully grown-up. We let them know that we are still there for guidance, support, and — most importantly — caring and love.

POWER STRUGGLES

I found the note on the dining room table: "I'm sorry, Mom and Dad, but I just have to get away. I'll call you." My oldest son had taken the battered car we had just given him and was driving from Boston to California, where he ended up staying with relatives. I was very angry, not so much at his leaving, but at the way he did it. If he had talked to me about what he wanted to do and made arrangements for regular communication, I probably would have agreed to the trip.

When I got over my initial anger and disappointment, my son's actions made more sense. As the oldest son, he had always been a conformist and was very authority-oriented. He worked hard at school and at his various part-time jobs. He had been a Boy Scout, taken piano lessons, and was a first-rate tennis player. He was mature, responsible, and — aside from keeping a messy room — had never given us a moment's worry. Perhaps, I thought, being a model child had taken its toll. Maybe he needed to break some rules and test some limits in order to assert himself and find his own identity.

The Search for Identity

Going off on a trip without permission is one of a number of actions teenagers may engage in for the purpose of self-discovery. Adolescents' power plays can range from experimenting with tobacco and alcohol to hanging out with the "wrong" crowd. Such actions are, in effect, tests of power: in each instance, a teenager challenges our parental rules and values as a way of establishing his or her own independence and individuality.

Renowned psychoanalyst Erik H. Erikson has described adolescence as a period during which young people need to establish a sense of personal identity. They must assemble their various social roles — as student, friend, sibling, grandchild — into some meaningful whole that makes sense. This sense of identity, or "meta-role," provides continuity with the past and guidance for the future.

In addition, teenagers have to construct their own value system — what they believe is right or wrong, good or bad, and so on. Adolescents cannot do this in a vacuum, but rather must do so through conflict and confrontation in a social arena. We parents are usually the primary contenders. It is only by challenging our rules and values that young people can discover what is right for them, as opposed to what they have accepted on the basis of our authority.

In such confrontations, teenagers are very sensitive to our prejudices and often focus upon these preconceived opinions. For example, if we have expressed negative feelings about a particular racial group or religion, our teenager may not only throw these prejudices back at us, but proceed to date a young person of that race, or attend religious services at the church we specified. By challenging us in this way, teenagers arrive at their own, independent evaluations of other races and religions.

Paradoxically, it is because young people need to confront our rules and values that it is so important for us to be firm about them (but not about our prejudices!). When we set clear rules and values, and are very explicit about the consequences for violating them, we give teenagers the framework they need to establish their own rules and values. On the other hand, if we are wishy-washy and do not take a strong stand, our teens cannot find anything against which to define themselves.

What Parents Can Do

Sometimes, of course, teenagers throw us a curve. They break a rule that we have left unspoken because we assumed it was understood and would not be violated. If the power play is not too serious, it is best to verbalize the rule and the consequences for breaking it in the future. We don't like after-the-fact punishments, nor do teens. If a power play is very serious, we need to express our displeasure, unhappiness, and disappointment with our teen's behavior. At the very least, this lets the teen know that his or her actions do have consequences — such as making us unhappy.

We have to understand that teenagers' power plays are not personal attacks on us or our authority. In some respects, it is actually a compliment to us that our teenagers engage in such defiant acts. It means that we have given them the confidence they need to establish their own sense of identity. And, once they become young adults, our offspring are likely to embrace many of the values and beliefs that we have modeled for them.

The process of forming an identity can also work both ways. Sometimes, in their defiance of our prejudices, teenagers can awaken us to our own shortcomings. Identity formation is never complete, and adolescents' efforts to understand themselves can help us parents better understand ourselves.

THE RIGHT TO PRIVACY

Writers keep journals. So, as an aspiring novelist, I started keeping a journal when I was 14. My journal included observations, snatches of conversations, turns of phrase, plot ideas, characters, and so on. During high school, I carried a small notebook with me to make entries during the school day.

My first mistake was taking my journal to a football game. My second mistake was making an entry in it when surrounded by curious teenagers. I heard an Apache shout, and then the notebook was grabbed out of my hands and tossed from one laughing hyena to another. My third mistake was trying to get it back. I ended up with a beaut of a shiner, a bloody nose, and an emasculated journal with only the cardboard end-papers remaining. What hurt the most, discounting the physical damage, was that my private world had been invaded.

The Emergence and Value of Privacy

For teenagers, the idea of having a private world of thoughts — which no one else shares — is new and precious. Until adolescence, we don't really think about our own ideas or realize that other people cannot read our minds. Entering the world of mental privacy gives us a wonderful, new sense of control over ourselves and our world.

While privacy is also important to adults, it is especially important to teenagers. The gradual construction of a inner world during the teenage years is one of the most important components of an adolescent's sense of personal identity. We learn a great deal about who and what we are through our private thoughts, feelings, and experiences, which we keep to ourselves for many different reasons. Some thoughts and feelings may be socially unacceptable; others might be hurtful or painful to someone else if expressed.

Psychoanalyst Erik Erikson argues that a sense of personal identity is a prerequisite to the establishment of inter-personal intimacy. Intimacy, in this sense, is much more than sexual. It is the readiness and willingness to share one's private world with another human being. This sharing of intimacies — of never-before-voiced feelings, thoughts, ambitions, heartaches, and heartbreaks — becomes the cement of abiding relationships.

What Parents Can Do

A teenager's privacy, then, should never be treated lightly. But, where does a teenager's right to privacy end and the parent's right to intrude begin? When it is a question of a teenager's diary or journal, which is kept as a matter of personal record, the teenager's privacy should be fully respected. The same is true for the teenager's phone conversations and his or her talks with friends and relatives. I would argue the same for the teenager's room and personal belongings.

However, the right to privacy, like all human rights, has limits. A teenager exceeds these limits when he or she misuses privacy to steal, abuse drugs, or deal drugs. If we discover that our teenager has misused privacy in this way, the rights to privacy have to be modified. We must make it clear that we will not tolerate the presence or use of drugs in the home, and that we will inspect rooms and belongings to make sure this rule is followed.

A more difficult situation arises when we suspect that our teen is stealing, or using or dealing drugs, but we have no real proof. Do we or do we not invade the teenager's privacy in search of evidence to support our concerns? I believe there is an intermediate step that we can take: we can sit down with our teenager and openly express our suspicions, as well as our concerns about the risks involved in these activities.

I believe that our general stance as parents should be one that respects and values teenagers' privacy, in the same way that we hope they will respect and value our own. At the same time, I think we should also make it clear that our teenagers can enjoy the freedom from intrusion into their privacy only as long as they abide by the responsibilities which accompany that freedom.

PREPARING TEENS
FOR A DIVORCE

Divorce is much more common and socially acceptable today than it was at mid-century. Nonetheless, experiencing a divorce is a little like breaking your leg on a ski trip: no matter how many other people at the lodge break their leg, your broken leg doesn't hurt any less. Divorce is always painful, regardless of how commonplace it has become.

Many parents believe that teens, because of their maturity and independence, can handle divorce better than younger children can. Some parents even delay divorce until their children are older, believing that it may be less traumatic. Research suggests, however, that delaying divorce may not have its intended beneficial effects. In her book, *Second Chances*, Judith Wallerstein describes the results of a study in which she followed divorced families for ten years. Among other findings, she reports that teens often have violent emotional reactions to their parents' divorce.

Parents of young children may be able to disguise the depth of their anger and grief at the breakup of their marriage, but it is difficult to deceive older children about such emotions. As a result, teenagers may become very anxious seeing their parents in such a vulnerable condition — particularly when the teens are feeling so vulnerable themselves. Wallerstein also found that the normal anxieties of adolescence are heightened by divorce, and that teenagers are often terrified that they will repeat their parents' failures. In addition, many teens feel rejected by both parents, who may be so wrapped up in their own problems that they have few emotional resources to expend on their offspring.

What Parents Can Do

It is best to tell your child about your plans to divorce as soon as the decision has been made. Since teenagers understand concepts such as custody, child support, and property division, you should be as open as possible about what arrangements will be made and how your child's life will be affected by them.

Parents should not, however, expect teenagers to handle the divorce with aplomb. Let your adolescent know that you realize this is a difficult time for him or her, too. Some teens try to mask their anger by affecting indifference. Others are openly hostile. Although your teenager's initial reaction may hurt you, eventually you and your teen can become sources of comfort and support for each other.

How well children involved in a divorce fare depends, in large part, on what type of relationship the parents are able to maintain during and after the divorce. While almost half of the children in Wallerstein's study experienced some lingering negative effects from their parents' divorce, children whose parents maintained a respectful relationship adjusted better than did those whose parents fought bitterly and used the children to vent their anger.

If the financial and custodial issues that will be part of the settlement cause family friction, professional assistance may be warranted. An outsider can look at the situation objectively and offer balanced advice, helping parents make decisions that are less hurtful to everyone involved.

HELPING TEENS AFTER A DIVORCE

Bud, a depressed teenager whom I was called in to evaluate, had been living with his father since his mother moved out. Bud was angry at his mother for having left his father, yet missed her very much. He also disliked and resented the new man in his mother's life. These feelings had affected Bud's school work, and left him with a sense of alienation both from school and from his peers. An average student before the separation, he was actually failing two courses the semester I evaluated him in connection with a dispute over joint custody. It was almost a year before he could get on with his life, raise his grades, and feel comfortable with his friends again.

Bud's reaction to his parents' divorce is fairly typical of his age group. In the book mentioned in the previous piece, *Second Chances,* Judith Wallerstein describes the short-term and long-term effects of divorce on teenagers. One of her findings is that "those who entered adolescence in the immediate wake of their parents' divorce had a particularly hard time...An alarming number of teenagers felt abandoned physically and emotionally." Wallerstein attributes this finding to the fact that teenagers are forming their first strong emotional attachments to the opposite sex and are beginning to fantasize about happy "forever-aftering" with a loving mate. It is difficult to maintain that kind of fantasy when parents divorce.

In addition, young people subconsciously assume that their parents will stay together and always be there to look after them. When that sense of protection is shaken, teenagers often wonder what will happen to them and who will take care of them. The future seems scary.

Many factors influence the way a teenager handles his or her parents' divorce. Some teenagers manage to forge ahead despite the divorce. Others, like Bud, are less resilient and go through a difficult period before they get on with their lives. As indicated in the previous piece, the nature of the parents' interaction during the divorce has a major impact on an adolescent's response. When a couple moves apart without recrimination, it is easier for the teenager than when the parents are hostile and demand that the teenager take sides. Teenagers who have understanding relatives and friends around to cushion the shock also fare better than those with little or no support.

What Parents Can Do

Once a divorce has occurred, parents need to do everything possible to reduce the stress on their offspring. If at all possible, teenage children should continue to live in the same house and attend the same school. The fewer life changes, aside from the absence of one parent, the less stress on the teens. Another means of reducing stress is for parents to avoid using their children to get back at each other. Perhaps most importantly, teenagers need to be told — not once, but many times — that their parents still love them.

GRANDPARENTS AND TEENAGERS

In her book, *Necessary Losses,* Judith Viorst describes her mother's changed role as a grandmother: "My mother had no dreams to lay on my children. She had tried...and succeeded...and failed with my sister and me. She was done with that now and her grandsons couldn't defeat her. Or disappoint her. Or prove anything — anything good or anything bad — about her. And I saw her free of ambition, free of the need to control, free of anxiety. Free, as she liked to put it — to enjoy."

Grandparents and teenagers often get along so well precisely because the grandparents do not need the teenagers' achievements to prove anything to themselves or to others. And, for teenagers, grandparents can be a sensitive sounding board for life plans, supportive listeners when fears of personal inadequacy or failure arise, and a wonderfully appreciative audience for performances and achievements.

While the relations between teenagers and their grandparents are usually close and positive, this closeness can sometimes present problems.

What Parents Can Do

For example, one teenager I know was very troubled when his grandfather remarried soon after his grandmother's death — without telling anyone about it beforehand. While grandparents certainly have a right to lead their own lives, we parents may need to remind them to think about the impact their decisions will have on grandchildren who feel close to them.

Another problem may arise when a teenager takes advantage of a grandparent's generosity. In one case, a teenage girl gave up her babysitting job and simply obtained her spending money from her grandmother. This violated an agreement she had made with her parents to earn her own spending money. The parents had to make it clear to both the teenager and the grandparent that this was a violation of an agreement and therefore needed to stop.

Relationships between teenagers and their grandparents can cause friction between the parents and grandparents in other ways, as well. Trouble may occur when a teen stays at the grandparents' home after school or during long parental vacations. As parents, we are likely to have ideas about diet, discipline, dress, or curfews that differ from those of our parents. One way to handle these differences is to agree that teenagers will follow their parents' rules when in their parents' home, and follow their grandparents' rules when in their grandparents' home. The only exception would be when the teen's health or well-being might be adversely affected. For example, if a teenager is diabetic, parents must insist that grandparents monitor the teen's diet while he or she is in their home.

There are also times when even those adolescents who have a very close relationship with their grandparents can be neglectful — particularly if the grandparents live far away.

We may need to remind teenagers to call or write their grandparents, and help the teens understand that grandparents want to be appreciated just as much as teenagers do.

LETTING GO

After a lecture in California last spring, a father came up to me and asked if I would answer a question that he preferred not to voice publicly. I agreed, and as we walked out together, he told me that his 16-year-old daughter had been asked to an overnight beach party by a boy she really liked. He opposed the idea strongly and was pleased to see the relief on his daughter's face when he said no. Later, he heard her talking to the boy on the phone, saying that she would love to go to the party but that her father wouldn't permit it. He felt comfortable about saying no, but he wondered whether his daughter should have said no on her own, rather than making him the ogre.

My reaction was that it is okay for a parent to play the ogre now and then. Had his daughter said no on her own, this could have been taken as a rejection, as an expression of fear or anxiety, or as something else entirely. Using her father as the explanation made it clear that the father cared enough about his daughter to take an unpopular stand, and that the daughter cared enough about her father to respect his wishes. Most adolescents can accept, admire, and perhaps even envy this kind of relationship. In my opinion, this was a case in which letting go — in the sense of making the daughter say no on her own — was not the wisest course of action.

Letting go is never a single event in which we launch — once and for all — a young person into adult life. In fact, we begin the process of letting go when our children are infants and probably never stop until we are gone. When we allow infants to feed themselves because they have demonstrated that they are capable of doing so, we have begun the process of granting freedom in return for a demonstration of competence and responsibility. When we finally permit a child to ride his or her bike in the street, or when we give our teenager the keys to the family car, we are gradually teaching the many ways in which freedom is tied to responsibility. And, it is through this schooling in the many ways each of us must take responsibility for our actions that we prepare young people to become independent adults.

What Parents Can Do

Helping an adolescent grow into independence and adulthood is much more an attitude than a technique or a strategy. There is no precise formula that will simplify our task of deciding when to hold tight, when to loosen our grip, and when to let go altogether. What will help us make the healthiest decision in every case is our commitment to the teenager's development as a person. If we try to distance ourselves from our own feelings and concerns, and ask ourselves what is best for the teenager, we are likely to do the right thing.

Sometimes, of course, we make mistakes, or young people do. Life is never an accident-free journey for anyone. At such times, we may feel tempted either to wash our hands of the matter, or to move in and take charge as we did when our children were small. However, I think we need to resist both tendencies. For example, if our teenager fails to keep an appointment, we should insist that he or she call and apologize. We should not do it ourselves, nor should we ignore the incident.

We never do (nor should) give up our parental role entirely. But, as our children mature, our relationship must change as well. While I don't believe we should be "pals" with our children, friendship with them becomes more natural as they leave the teenage years. And, being friends with them does not mean that we deny our parenthood, because these young adults are more than just friends — they are our children, and we love them in a very special way. Being friends with them means that we acknowledge their adult status and that a new relationship is in order.

It is the establishment of this new relationship of mutual respect and caring between independent individuals that is the true mark of letting go. And, one of the nice things about it is that when we enter into this new relationship with our children, we often discover that our grown children now seek our advice and guidance — the same advice and guidance they once so staunchly resisted!

4
EDUCATION

OVERVIEW

In discussing the educational issues facing adolescents and their parents, it is helpful to distinguish between education in the *narrow* sense and education in the *broad* sense. In the narrow sense, education refers to all the knowledge, skills, and values that we learn in an academic setting. In contrast, education in the broad sense includes all that we learn within and without the school walls. In this chapter, I would like to consider educational issues in the broad rather than the narrow sense.

When we view education from a broader perspective, we can shift our focus from what teenagers are being taught to what it is that they are learning. During adolescence, much of what young people are learning has to do with their own abilities and their limitations, and those of the people around them. This personal and inter-personal learning — which teenagers may acquire through homework, summer activities, or applying to college, as well as in the classroom — constitutes a vital part of a young person's educational experience, even if it is not academic. In fact, developing this understanding of themselves and other people can be as important in preparing for success in life as any information contained in textbooks and courses. That is why this chapter includes pieces about topics which are not strictly school-related, but contribute to a discussion about education in the broad sense.

Reading is an appropriate starting point for any discussion about education. It is a many-splendored skill that serves as a vital means of education, a source of pleasure and recreation, and a tool required in almost every occupation. Helping young people develop a love of reading enhances their education and is one of the most important gifts we can provide. Homework is also important — not by itself, but in the context of an academic environment where there are high standards and expectations for students. However, homework can become an emotional lighting rod for issues that have nothing to do with school, so as parents we need to know when and how to become involved with it.

At times, we also need to take the difficult step of allowing our teenager to risk and even experience failure. One reason is that what seems like failure to us may not seem so to an adolescent. Some young people gain more from having tried and lost than from never having tried at all. Others surprise us and become successful in areas where we were sure that they would fail. On the other hand, some young people fail because they simply haven't made the effort. Allowing teenagers to experience the consequences of their own actions or inaction can be a very valuable lesson.

Another reason for discussing education in the broad sense is that schools have increasingly broadened the functions they perform for adolescents. In addition to feeding students, counseling them, and providing vocational training, many schools are now providing a variety of health services. While we might not object to schools providing routine health care for teenagers, some of us may object to school clinics providing birth control information and condoms. To a large extent, however, these and other new functions are being performed by the schools because so many parents no longer perform them. If we don't want the schools to be involved in these aspects of our children's lives, we parents have to do more in the way of sex education and counseling at home.

There are other ways in which schools now perform what were once family functions. Many schools are becoming community centers that provide social activities, which can contribute to teenagers' education in both the broad and narrow senses. In schools where there is a sense of community — particularly religious schools — teens tend do better than they do in schools without a sense of community. While a school may not foster a sense of community even though it provides many different services, it has been argued that the sense of community established in some schools provides young people with a form of "social capital" which contributes to academic achievement.

Two other important issues related to education in the broad sense involve adolescents with special needs and adolescents who are not athletically inclined. It is hard to put into words the extent of the difficulties experienced by children who have special needs. In addition to physical pain and anxiety, there is also the social pain and anxiety of having to deal with a physically fit society. While neither special-needs teens nor their parents can do so alone, together they can find the courage and spirit to overcome the difficulties of being outside the physical norm. A different kind of pain is experienced by teenagers who are not athletic. Particularly for boys, this can be a humiliating and ego-deflating experience. There are ways to cope, however, and ways for parents to help.

The summer months are not usually regarded as an educational period in the narrow sense, but they certainly can be educational in the broad sense. Although there has been much discussion about having year-round schools, a number of practical difficulties will prevent this approach from being widely implemented in the near future. In the meantime, there are a number of ways we can help our teenagers make their summers both enjoyable and educational.

For an increasing number of adolescents, high school is no longer the end of formal education. More than 50 percent of high school graduates now go on to college. So, most teenagers now have to decide whether or not to apply to college, and if they choose to apply, which colleges to apply to. The application process can be a very stressful time for teenagers, especially those who apply to prestigious colleges where the chances of acceptance are not high. We can help to reduce the stress for our prospective college students by emphasizing that many schools provide an excellent education, and that regardless of the school, a student will only obtain from a college education what he or she puts into it.

As to how much or how little we should participate in the selection and application process, usually it is more helpful to adolescents if we offer encouragement and support for what they are doing, rather than take a more direct and assertive role. While we may need to intervene more actively with some teenagers than with others, we have to accept the fact that adolescents are making a transition into adulthood and increasingly will have to make — and abide by — their own decisions. This is particularly true when it comes to making choices about whether to go to college and which college to attend. We can and should offer advice and counsel, but the final decision has to be made by the adolescent.

An important goal for both parents and teenagers is to appreciate the value of education in the broad sense, as well as in the narrow sense. Whenever we are talking about a topic related to education, we need to emphasize the importance of what is being learned, rather than just the grades or status involved.

A second goal, related to the first, is to help our teenagers understand that education in the broad sense is a life-long activity, for we only stop learning when we stop living. Young people who value learning for its own sake, and who regard it as a continuing activity, have an orientation that will stand them in good stead no matter what career they choose to pursue.

CUDDLE UP WITH
A GOOD BOOK

I recently spent some time in a local bookstore, hanging out around the Young Adult section. To my surprise, I saw a group of leather-jacketed, chain-rattling teenagers congregate around one of the sections. They were actually taking books off the shelves, opening them, and talking about them! When I moved closer, I saw that the books were about rock music and rock stars.

As Shakespeare might have said, "Some people are born readers, some people become readers, and some people have reading thrust upon them." Born — or *true* – readers read for personal growth and enlightenment, as well as for instruction, information, and entertainment. The majority of literate people are *functional* readers, who read primarily for information, instruction, or entertainment. The leather-jacketed teens in the bookstore fall within this category. Finally, there are *nominal* readers, who limit their reading to the minimum necessary to get by in our society.

By far the largest number of adolescents fall into the category of functional readers. Our job as parents is to come up with books that they will find interesting enough to read. Reading requires effort, and functional readers will expend this effort only on books that cater to their interests.

Some parents object to this suggestion because they feel that such books have little redeeming value. They would much prefer that their teenagers read books that have literary merit. While I share and appreciate this sentiment, I have learned in working with young people of all ages that it is best to start from where they are, rather than where I would like them to be. This holds true for reading. The most important thing is to get the young person reading, even if the material is not quite what we would wish.

Today's book scene for teenagers offers a healthier balance between solid fiction and message-oriented stories than was the case in the 1960's and 1970's. What has re-emerged for teenage girls, though, are romantic novels. Some of these are fluff (for example, Francine Pascal's *Sweet Valley High* series). Others, such as those written by Madeleine L'Engle (*A Swiftly Tilting Planet, A Wind in the Door*) and Barbara Brenner (*A Killing Season*), are much more substantial. Among teenage boys and some girls, there has been an explosion of interest in science fiction. The *Dune* series by Frank Herbert is one of the better-written examples of this genre.

Both teenage boys and girls enjoy well-written biographies and autobiographies, because these accounts give them ideas about how other adolescents went about forging a sense of personal identity — the task with which they themselves are preoccupied. Lindbergh's *The Spirit of St. Louis* and Anne Frank's *The Diary of a Young Girl* are books of this type that have retained their appeal for adolescent readers over many decades.

What Parents Can Do

Beyond encouraging our teenagers' reading by finding books that reflect their interests, is there anything else we can do to help adolescents to become more active, avid readers? I think there is, but we shouldn't wait until our children are half-grown. It is very important for us as parents to turn the television off, help our children obtain library cards, and make sure that they use them. And, because children learn best by example, if we are true readers or avid functional readers, we can be pretty sure that our offspring will be, as well.

When we model reading in our own behavior and help our children discover the wonders of reading from a very early age, they will carry this orientation into adolescence and adulthood. But, even if we did not do this when our children were small, it is never too late to limit television watching, to help a teenager obtain a library card, or to model reading. Young people can discover the pleasures and benefits of reading at any age.

HOMEWORK: WHEN TO INTERVENE

There are a thousand different homework stories in the city (as well as in the suburbs and rural areas). In *The Private Life of the American Teenager* by Jane Norman and Myron Harris, the parents and teens interviewed had no trouble recalling a few.

"If you say to your parents, 'Oh I have so much work to do' they won't say, 'Oh, that's too bad.' They say, 'Well, do it.' You want to express the fact that you're really bogged down and you can't stand it, but you can't get across to them because you know that once you tell them, they'll keep nagging you to do it." (Miriam, 17 years)

"When I say, 'I know you have a lot of work to do,' she takes this as permission not to do her homework." (Parent)

"My parents don't give me a hard time because they know that if I don't work, it's my problem. If they bugged me about it, I'd probably resent it and end up studying less." (Monica, 13 years)

"Thank God, I don't have a problem with my kids; they come, do their homework and chores, and then go out to spend time with their friends." (Parent)

The reason homework becomes a "story" for so many teenagers and their parents is that it is frequently transformed into a battleground for dealing with a variety of issues that have little or nothing to do with homework. Anger and resentment at the teenager for not doing his or her share of the household chores, or for hurtful words said in anger, can all be loaded into the demand that the teenager do his or her homework. The teenager, in turn, can express anger and resentment at the parents for a multitude of sins by not doing homework. When homework becomes a no-man's-land filled with negative feelings between a parent and a teen, it has lost its educational value.

In contemporary America, homework is often talked about as if it helps adolescents acquire a set of work habits and discipline over and above the particular skills and knowledge the teenager learns while doing the homework. There is absolutely no evidence, however, that homework in and of itself has any special educational benefits. On the other hand, when homework is part of an educational program that emphasizes academic achievement, and which requires students to complete a required basic curriculum, it can be effective.

A 1990 study supported this contention, when it compared schools with high academic expectations and standards (including regular homework) with schools that had low academic expectations and standards (and less homework). The results indicated that schools with high academic expectations and standards (of which homework was a part) graduated many more students than did schools which had lower expectations and standards (and less homework). In short, the benefits of homework are very much dependent upon the educational context of which it is a part.

What Parents Can Do

Given the fact that homework is often an emotional battle-field, and that its benefits depend upon the academic orientation of the school, should we ignore homework alto-gether? Not at all. But, we do have to be discriminating both with respect to the homework and to the particular teenager we are dealing with.

Homework is not an absolute good. As we have seen, homework has the most value if it is part of an academic system with high overall academic expectations and stan-dards. If our teenager is in such an educational setting, it is important for us as parents to be persistent in voicing our expectations that the teenager does the homework before going out or watching television.

On the other hand, if homework — for whatever reason — has become overloaded with emotional debris related to other family matters, it is best to let it drop. What is more important is to deal with the other issues for which home-work has become an emotional lighting rod. Until those matters are resolved, insisting that a teenager do his or her homework will only incite an argument. Parental interven-tion in regard to homework can only be effective when it is free of unrelated family issues.

HOMEWORK:
HOW TO INTERVENE

By the time your adolescent reaches high school, you should be less involved in his or her homework. It's fine to ask about assignments — in fact, that's one way to keep informed about your teenager's education. Whether you should do anything more, such as actively monitoring homework assignments, depends on how the teen is doing in school.

It's best to work out a homework arrangement with a teenager at the beginning of the school year. Help your teen set priorities so that he or she can complete assignments and still spend time with friends, participate in after-school programs, and watch favorite TV shows.

Whether or not your teenager has homework, it's a good idea to set aside a time period each evening during which the television set and the phone are off-limits. If your adolescent doesn't have homework, he or she can spend the time reading a book or a newsmagazine. Keeping this time set aside will be easier if everyone in the family — not just your teen — reads or participates in some quiet activity.

If you set a minimum-time standard, it may encourage your teen to begin his or her work ahead of time and start studying for tests well in advance, rather than waiting until the night before. Once you've done this, it should be up to the teen to complete assignments. As long as he or she is doing well in school, there's no need for further involvement. You don't have to check on work or demand that more time be spent on it.

What Parents Can Do

Of course, if your teen's grades aren't up to par, or a teacher complains about the quality of his or her work, you should intervene. Nagging, threats, and bribery, however, tend not to be effective and can be counter-productive. You also want to be sure, as discussed in the previous section, that homework is just homework — not a lighting rod for other emotional matters. If you are dealing strictly with a homework issue, you may want to supervise homework assignments by making sure that they are finished on time and in reasonably good shape.

One parent I know was concerned about his 15-year-old son's performance in school. Whenever either parent asked Dan about his homework, he said it was already finished or that he didn't have any that night. When Dan received his report card, it was full of mediocre grades. Dan's parents told him that his performance had to improve and that they were going to monitor his work until it did. Dan became very upset and told his parents that they were treating him like a baby. They agreed that he could have another term to improve his grades without their involvement. Dan went to work, and his grades improved on his next report card.

This approach won't always work, but there are other options if we want or need to stay out of the homework story. One option is to engage a college student to serve as a tutor for an adolescent. Teenagers are often impressed by college students, and may take directions and suggestions from them that they would never take from us. With homework, as with many other matters, we often help our teen best by not becoming directly involved in an activity that is their responsibility.

LETTING KIDS FAIL

Recently, after giving a talk at a teacher's conference, I was seated next to a retired principal. In my lecture, I had spoken about not putting inappropriate pressures on young people. While he said that he agreed with me in most cases, he felt there were exceptions and offered an example. He told me about his son, who had been born with a clubfoot and had undergone a number of operations to correct the condition. The boy wanted to play ice hockey, and his parents were tempted to discourage him because they didn't want him to experience the disappointment of not making the team. Nonetheless, they supported his practicing and encouraged him to give it his all. Eventually, he did try out, and not only did he make the team, he went on to become a star player.

The Risks and Rewards of Failure

At times, we may discourage our teen's efforts because we believe they are likely to result in failure. Yet, for a teenager, exploration of and experimentation with abilities and talents is part of establishing an understanding of oneself and an identity. A friend's daughter tried out for the school marching band despite the fact that, as her mother put it, "She couldn't twirl a baton if her life depended on it!" The girl needed to give it a try for personal reasons; the risk of failure was less important to her than having made the effort. Similarly, the 115-pound young man who tries out for quarterback does so to reinforce his sense of self, regardless of what the outcome might be.

Why is making the effort, even when it seems destined to fail, so important to teenagers? In part, it comes from their need to feel like a member of an admired peer group, even if only briefly. For a moment or two, my friends' daughter felt like she *was* a member of the marching band; the young man who tried out for the football team experienced the fleeting thrill of being on the team. And, sometimes, as happened with the hockey player, a teenager can surprise everyone and attain a seemingly impossible goal.

There are other instances in which an adolescent flirts with failure not to test his limits or abilities, but rather to test adult resolve. For instance, a teenager who puts off doing a class project until the last minute, and then cannot finish it in time, tests both his parents and his teachers. If the teen knows that not turning in the project promptly will lower his grade, and if he has been reminded of this, then he needs to receive the lower grade. It may be the best way for him to learn that he is not exempt from the rules which govern everyone else.

What Parents Can Do

Our tendency as parents is to want to shield our child from the pain of failure. Nevertheless, there are occasions when we must allow adolescents to experience failure, in order for them to satisfy personal needs. Growing up is not always easy, but sometimes teenagers — not their parents — are the best judges of how to go about it.

When teens attempt an activity in which the risks of failure are great, we can support them by saying something like, "You know that the odds are against you, but if you believe that you can do it, go for it! We're with you all the way."

Of course, a teenager may work very hard with the expectation of success, but fail nonetheless. At such times, it is important to say something such as, "You gave it your best shot — that's all you can do, and that is the most important thing you can do. It would have been nice if you had won, but what counts is the time and effort you put in, and what you learned from that. I am really proud of you."

At other times, teenagers may fail, not despite their best efforts, but because they made little or no effort. In these situations, it is tempting to say "I told you so." A more positive approach is to say something like, "I am as unhappy about this as I'm sure you are, and I really will be pleased if you do a better job next time." Although an adolescent's failure to perform is serious, we should not give up on the young person. We need to say instead that we really believe he or she can — and will — do better in the future.

PHYSICAL EDUCATION

"Elkind? Ugh!" was the disgusted refrain that greeted me as I walked across the gymnasium floor to join a team whose visibly unhappy captain had just chosen me over "roly-poly" Arthur. Many schools have a particularly barbaric ceremony for making up sports teams in gym class. A number of team leaders are chosen, and the leaders — usually stellar athletes — then take turns selecting players from among the remaining students seated on the gymnasium floor. The least athletic students are always chosen last. And, these poor unfortunates become increasingly conspicuous as the teams grow larger and the number of seated students grows smaller and smaller.

As excruciating as this experience can be for any young person, it is particularly painful for teenage boys, whose participation in sports is a primary path to social acceptance. Boys' friendships often center around athletics, as sports provide not only a common bond, but also a common vocabulary and an endless topic of conversation.

Participation in sports is much less central to friendships and social acceptance for adolescent girls. Friendships established among teenage girls tend to be more complex and multi-leveled, often centering around personalities, interests, tastes, and appearance, rather than sports.

Unathletic and Athletic Teens

Some teenagers are simply poor at sports. This can be the result of a lack of motor coordination, which can prove frustrating and discourage a young person from participating in athletics. Other teenagers simply have no interest in athletic activities of any kind. And, still others are reluctant to participate in sports because they believe their bodies are ugly and they do not want to be ridiculed.

It was not until I became an adult that I learned my own problem with ball sports was one of visual rather than motor coordination. I was, however, fortunate to find a sport — swimming — which I could do well in and enjoy. One option for the unathletic teenager, then, is to look for a sport in which he or she can find both pleasure and success. It's important, too, to convey the message that a person doesn't have to be — or look like — a star athlete to feel good about his or her body.

With a teenager who *is* a star athlete, parents may have different causes for concern, such as the possibility of the teen becoming obsessed with sports. A young man or woman who is a talented athlete usually excels in many different sports. For this sort of adolescent, questions arise as to how many sports to participate in and how much time to devote to each of them. And, there is really no simple answer. As a general rule, if the teenager is doing well in both studies and in sports, there may be no problem. But, for many talented athletes, participation in sports can sometimes get out of hand.

I know of one young man who was on the wrestling, football, and swimming teams. He was spending so much time practicing and going to meets and games that his grades began to suffer. At my suggestion, his parents insisted that he choose one sport and give the others up. Although he was reluctant to do so at first, he ended up choosing one and was then able to devote more time to his studies, while still enjoying athletic pursuits.

What Parents Can Do

Whether a teenager is a stellar athlete devoted to sports, or the last-picked kid in the gym class, it is important for us as parents to emphasize that athletics should be fun and exhilarating — a way to exercise and feel better about oneself. The best way to encourage teenagers along these lines is through our own actions. If we exercise regularly, even if only to take long walks, we are setting a good example for our children — one that can benefit them throughout their lives.

SCHOOL HEALTH CLINICS

"Daily, Barbara Taylor counsels...teenage students who come to the convenient in-school health clinic located on the main floor of Central High School in St. Paul, Minnesota...The help students seek can be for acute illness, dental problems, or obesity. Sometimes, it is for a range of other reasons; violence in the home, boy-girl relationships, sexual counseling, emotional problems, incest, problems with parents, pregnancy..." according to a newsletter from Healthy Children, a program encouraging the development of children's health services.

In the St. Paul in-school health clinic — as in the more than 115 other such clinics in various states — many teenagers are provided with a range of health services that would otherwise be unavailable to them. Teenagers whose parents are unable to afford a private physician often don't see a doctor for anything other than the most critical of health problems. Other youngsters — whose parents do not themselves seek regular, preventive health care — may be unlikely to see a physician or pediatrician unless an inexpensive one is readily accessible to them. Due to the growing number of children in situations such as these, the American Academy of Pediatrics recently issued a statement supporting the selective implementation of school-based health clinics in areas where the health-care needs of the school-age population are not being met.

Because of the current concern about teenage pregnancy and AIDS, some clinics have also begun to offer sexual counseling, contraceptive information, and, sometimes, contraceptives. This extension of in-school health services to sexual well-being has created a great deal of controversy. Many people favor in-school health clinics providing sexual counseling and contraceptives because of evidence showing that such provisions are effective both in delaying the age at which some teenagers become sexually active, and in reducing the number of teenage pregnancies. Yet, other groups — for moral and religious reasons — are opposed to sexual counseling and the distribution of contraceptives.

Providing general health care — including immunization against disease — in the schools is not the same as providing sexual counseling, contraceptive information, and contraceptives. The first is a medical service that is appropriately provided by health professionals, while the second involves moral and religious values, as well as health concerns. Virtually all parents are likely to agree that there are benefits when schools provide immunizations and health information regarding something like nutrition, but parents in any community are likely to be sharply divided as to whether or not schools should provide sexual counseling and contraceptives.

Public schools, to the best of their ability, must not reflect any particular moral or religious orientation, while being supportive of universal moral standards and of all religions. When in-school clinics provide a service that goes against the moral or religious beliefs of a large percentage of parents, it puts the other services they provide and the clinics themselves at risk. Unfortunately, this is the case with sexual counseling and contraceptives.

What Parents Can Do

These are not easy issues to resolve. But, as parents, we can do what I have suggested elsewhere in this book: talk openly with our teenagers about sexual activity, explaining its risks as well as its pleasures. If we effectively provide this sort of information and counseling at home, there will be less need for it in the schools.

GIVE ME THAT
OLD-TIME RELIGION

How can we improve the educational achievements of teen-agers? A solution being tried in some parts of the country is to raise standards, increase homework, and lengthen the school day or school year.

A somewhat different and unheralded solution is suggested by James S. Coleman and Thomas Hoffer in their recent book, *Public and Private High Schools: The Impact of Communities.* They begin with the finding that students in Catholic and other private schools showed higher achievement in mathematics and verbal skills than did public school students who had comparable backgrounds.

Another finding reinforced the first. Over a two-year period, the dropout rate in public schools for grades ten to twelve was 14.3 percent. In Catholic schools, however, the dropout rate was 3.4 percent, and in other religiously homogeneous schools (Jewish, Baptist, and other Christian denominations) the dropout rate was about 3.7 percent.

In reviewing these and other findings, Coleman and Hoffer concluded that it was not Catholicism or any other religion, per se, that accounted for the higher achievement and lower dropout rates. Rather, what seemed to make a difference was the *sense of community* that pervaded the religious school and influenced the students and their families. This secure sense of community, growing out of an intricate support system, provided what Coleman and Hoffer termed "social capital," which the student and his or her family could draw upon in times of need.

It is important to separate the concept of being part of a religious community from that of having a particular religious affiliation. A teenager and his or her family can belong to a religious community without regular attendance at a church or a synagogue. Indeed, many teenagers take a sabbatical from institutional religion, particularly during the early adolescent years. But, this in no way means that these teens have left the church, synagogue, or other religious community. The religion of teenagers is a highly personal one. God is often seen as a close friend — a wise confidant to whom one can reveal one's most fearful and shameful thoughts, with the secure knowledge that God won't "squeal."

Many religious institutions wisely play down formal religious instruction and practice during the early and middle teenage years, focusing instead on social skills and activities. This sort of emphasis keeps adolescents within the religious community, without intruding upon their highly personal religious relationship.

What Parents Can Do

The Coleman and Hoffer concept of social capital reaffirms the common-sense view of community. That is, living in a supportive environment which has clear-cut standards and values promotes healthy growth and development — including academic achievement — among young people.

Many of us, however, are not fortunate enough to be part of such a religious community. In some cases, we may even harbor some antipathy to institutional religion. What should we do then?

Social capital can come from many different forms of community. For example, a large, extended family wherein there are many uncles, aunts, and cousins can provide a great deal of social capital. Social organizations, such as Young Farmers of America, can provide support groups and serve as a source of social capital for youth. In our public schools, the current movement toward "cooperative" learning may help students attain a better sense of community, in addition to helping them learn more effectively and improve their social skills. The religious community is only one of the communities from which an adolescent can draw social capital.

The research demonstrating the value of social capital refutes those who argue that individual competitiveness is the key to success in our society. Quite to the contrary, we are social beings, and we need to work effectively with other people. The positive effects of social capital show just how important cooperation and support networks are for adolescents.

SUMMER PROJECTS

From the age of 14 until I turned 21 and graduated from college, I spent every summer working as a busboy at my uncle's resort hotel in the Catskill Mountains in upstate New York. On my days off, I took a bus into Manhattan, went to a movie, and had dinner at a Chinese restaurant. One day, I discovered the Barnes & Noble Bookstore on 18th Street. It was huge, or so it seemed to me at the time, and had a vast used-book section. There were all the classics at bargain prices. Soon, I was spending entire days off on 18th Street (I did not, however, forego the Chinese dinner!) and ended up lugging tons of books back to the hotel with me. Going to a used-book store may not seem very exciting unless you are a bookworm like me — then it is endlessly fascinating.

To be truly enjoyable and challenging, as my experience indicates, a summer project has to grow out of a teenager's own interests and activities. It is a form of self-discovery that is educational in the broad sense that it can help an adolescent make better choices about his or her life. Unfortunately, developing this sort of project is not quite as easy as it sounds.

Many of today's teenagers have not had the opportunity to find out what they truly enjoy. In part, this has happened because entertainment is so constantly available — via, for example, portable tape players. Perhaps, today's young people become accustomed from an early age to being entertained rather than entertaining themselves. That may be why certain teenagers are often "bored."

David Rapaport, a Freudian scholar, argued that when external stimulation is too constant, we lose touch with our inner world and become slaves to the outer world. This is what happens when someone is brainwashed. The stimulation coming from the environment is so constant that the victim loses touch with his or her inner self. As a result, the person becomes a virtual automaton.

To be sure, teenagers are not robots. I do believe, however, that many contemporary adolescents have sacrificed some of their autonomy — their ability to respond to their inner world — because they are so constantly bombarded by television and music.

Regaining Autonomy

There are many different ways teenagers can regain their autonomy. Meditation and prayer, for example, are universal and time-honored techniques for getting in touch with our inner selves. Taking walks — without earplugs — is another way in which teens can get acquainted with their inner thoughts and feelings. A very useful way of regaining autonomy is keeping a diary, because writing about the day's events provides an opportunity for us to reflect upon our motives and actions.

One major project for the summer might be for a teenager to find an autonomy-regaining activity, such as one of those described above, and pursue it for the duration of the summer (and, hopefully, beyond). Learning about ourselves is the first and most important step toward finding recreational and vocational pursuits that are meaningful and rewarding. It is also a prerequisite for making the best possible choices in regard to one's education.

What Parents Can Do

In addition to encouraging young people to engage in some regular self-discovery activities, we might also make other suggestions. A healthy counter-point to the introspective activities described above is community service. For example, at least a few young people I know spend some time each week talking with, reading to, or writing for an elderly person. Other teenagers volunteer to clean up a beach or a park area.

For sheer fun, many teenagers enjoy taking bicycle trips to other cities or hiking trips through mountains. Parents should, of course, monitor these plans and make sure that an older, experienced person is overseeing the expedition.

However teenagers spend their summers, they will enjoy and profit from their experiences most if they take time for themselves, as well as give some time to others. In this way, an adolescent develops the healthy sense of balance between self-realization and community service which is so essential to a happy and productive life.

TEENS WITH SPECIAL NEEDS

Recently, I spent an afternoon with a group of teenagers who have spina bifida, a deforming disease of the spine. They were splashing around and enjoying themselves in the swimming pool of the university hospital where they receive treatment and participate in an educational program. Later on, I talked with them about how they were separated from their peers, and whether they would like to attend a regular high school instead. I received the impression that they preferred to stay together as a group.

This preference illustrates their vulnerability. Adolescents believe that they are constantly on stage. Because of this self-consciousness, teenagers are very sensitive to the reactions of others, which makes life especially difficult for teens with special needs. As children, many of these youngsters are happy to be "mainstreamed" in regular classrooms, where they are achieving, courageous kids. As teenagers, however, they wonder what other people think of their appearance and often distrust expressions of friendship, interpreting these well-meant gestures as unwelcome expressions of pity. Because they are so self-conscious, disabled teens often prefer to socialize with other disabled young people who share and understand their problems.

For this reason, mainstreaming teenagers with special needs into regular high school classrooms may not always be the best educational decision. If we cannot guarantee these adolescents a sensitive, understanding, and supportive school setting, they may be best served by a special class or school, especially during their early teen years. Each teenager with special needs should be consulted as to his or her preferences, as the teens themselves are usually the best judges of their own needs and vulnerabilities.

What Parents Can Do

Having a disabled child is one of the heaviest burdens a parent can bear. I know this to be true from personal experience — one of my children has had a series of life-threatening illnesses.

We all want so much for our children: we want them to be happy, liked, appreciated, and successful in whatever they want to do. Those of us who are parents of children with special needs often wish that their disabilities had been visited on us rather than on them. We feel abiding hurt when we cannot make things right and have to watch our children struggle. Although we feel heartened by their courage and resourcefulness, we also grieve at their occasional signs of despair. All our love, support, and encouragement cannot wipe away the reality these young people confront every morning.

Ultimately, there is only one healthy solution — the one that my own son taught me — acceptance. Once he gave up asking "Why me?" and comparing himself with others, he was able to get on with his life. And, what a rich life it is!

For me — and I believe for most parents of children with special needs — a young person's acceptance lessens the guilt but not the pain. That pain is one of the prices we gladly pay for the many gifts that our special children bring us.

STUDENTS' DECISIONS ABOUT COLLEGE

"Oooh, Elkind, sooo dumb!" was a refrain I heard often during our lunchtime game of hearts at Dorsey High School in Los Angeles. An indifferent student, I was an even more indifferent card player and always failed to count or — more often — counted incorrectly, so that I invariably was stuck with the "Black Queen." In my senior year, perhaps with "Sooo dumb!" seared into my brain, I set out to discover whether or not I was as dumb as I was purported to be. I did well, and my performance encouraged me to go on to college, which neither I nor my family had seriously considered. Once at UCLA, I "found" myself as a student and went on to pursue a rewarding academic career.

I tell this story not — or at least not entirely — to work through the traumatic experience of those high school years, but to make a point about going to college. Academic performance is determined by many different factors. Although high school performance is usually a pretty good predictor of how a young person will do in college, this is not always the case. Some adolescents who do very well in high school do poorly in college, while the reverse — as in my case — is also not unusual. In short, all is not over if a student has not done particularly well in high school. A year or two in a community college, or a couple of evening courses, will sometimes reveal that a mediocre high school student has the "right stuff" for college work.

The "Best Fit"

For those students who do well in high school and who have their sights set on college, choosing the right one is a complex decision. Ideally, the decision should be based on finding the "best fit" or match between the young person's abilities, interests, and personality, and the college's characteristics. This requires a little research about colleges, and some consideration of the student's interests and goals.

Choosing which colleges to apply to is much easier for students with definite interests and career goals, who can identify and apply to appropriate colleges. Other students, perhaps the majority, are less certain of their career goals. Such students may want to keep their occupational options open and explore different areas of interest before committing themselves to a definite course of study. This is a reasonable and adaptive position, especially given the changing nature of career opportunities these days.

Size may also be a consideration. Some students are intimidated by large universities and feel more comfortable in the family atmosphere of the small liberal arts college. Other students relish the anonymity and diversity provided by a large university.

Cost, of course, is a major consideration when choosing a college. Fortunately, most colleges and universities now have scholarships for students who qualify for financial aid. Competition for these awards is becoming greater, however, and a student should apply for several rather than just one. When appropriate, it is also important to check on special awards available to students of a particular ethnic back-ground, or those who have special talents or handicaps.

What Parents Can Do

Choosing a college is, in many ways, a major step toward independence from the family. Most teenagers want and need to make this decision on their own. We can help by taking them on a tour of some of the colleges they are con-sidering, and by helping in any way we can with the application process. We can and should also present our best estimate as to which schools our teen might find most re-warding. But, we need to present our judgments as information the young person can use in making his or her decision, not as the path the student has to follow.

After a student has decided on a college and is in atten-dance, he or she may discover that the experience is not really working out as planned or hoped for. In some cases, it then makes sense to switch schools. We should be support-ive of this decision when it is made on substantial grounds and involves a realistic acknowledgement that the school was a wrong choice. We all make mistakes, and students are no exceptions. The majority of students who switch schools do as well or better at the new school. And, one important lesson young people can learn from changing schools with our support is that they do not have to remain in a bad situation.

COLLEGES' DECISIONS ABOUT STUDENTS

From a college admission officer's perspective, how important are your teenager's SAT scores, high school grades, extracurricular activities, application essays, and recommendations?

Although policies vary from school to school, applicants and parents may be reassured to know that admissions officers from public and private colleges and universities say that they consider each of these components separately, and that no single part of an application either guarantees or rules out a student's admission.

The academic record is generally the most important part of a student's application, because it provides a long-term picture of his or her abilities, rather than the "snapshot" available from a one-day test. Which courses a student has taken are also considered, as a student who received all A's in courses such as typing and music appreciation will be ranked lower than a student who had some B's but received them in physics, calculus, and English literature. An academic record of steady improvement is usually regarded more favorably than one that is erratic or shows a pattern of decline.

Admissions officers also report that the importance of SAT and ACT scores is somewhat exaggerated. But, they add that such scores are useful because they are the only standardized measurement with which to compare students from different parts of the country, or from schools with different academic standards.

The quality of a student's extracurricular activities tends to be more important than the quantity. For example, a student who has a commitment to environmental causes and spends his free time working for these causes is likely to be ranked higher than, say, a student who has participated in a number of different activities but shows no clear commitment to any particular one.

Interviews, essays, and letters of recommendation are most important for borderline cases. A candidate who comes across as more articulate in person than on paper may help his cause. In the same way, a particularly good essay or strong letter of recommendation from a high school teacher can also strengthen an application that is less impressive in other respects.

What Parents Can Do

Trying to put the application process in perspective is helpful for all concerned. While you are living through this process, it may seem overwhelmingly important that your teenager select the "right" school and that the "right" school select him or her. But, try to keep in mind that this is just one in a series of steps that adolescents take on their way to completing their formal education.

Nevertheless, there is no anxiety quite so excruciating for a high school senior as waiting for the mail during the college-admission season. A fat envelope — filled with forms to fill out — shouts acceptance. A thin one whispers rejection.

If the results are not what your teenager wanted, try to be sensitive to the feelings of disappointment and embarrassment that are sure to follow. A rejection is a blow to the self-esteem of even the most laid-back teenager. It is especially important at this time that your teen knows that you love and believe in him or her, no matter what any academic institution has decided. And, it is also important for you to keep in mind that a rejection is not a reflection on your success as a parent.

Help your child take strength from the truth that, in the end, we are measured not by the schools we attend, but rather by what we *do* with the education we receive.

5
ADAPTING TO SOCIETY

OVERVIEW

In their transition to adulthood, adolescents are afforded many new freedoms and responsibilities, which are part of becoming full-fledged members of our society. During this process, teenagers must learn to deal with the freedom to engage in actions that can be pleasurable in the short term but self-destructive in the long term. In addition, teens must learn about the dark side of society — those people who are ready to take advantage of an individual's sense of trust and loyalty. Ideally, adolescents should also find meaningful ways to make their own contributions to the larger society of which they are becoming a part.

Like so many other aspects of parenting teenagers, our task of helping teenagers cope with these new freedoms and responsibilities is not easy. We have to encourage young people to be more independent and accept their new responsibilities. But, at the same time we also have to set limits in order to help our adolescents appreciate that their new freedoms are earned privileges, and not simply rights automatically granted them on their attainment of puberty. In other words, we have to find some middle ground between supporting independence and fostering a sense of social responsibility.

This is more difficult today than it was at mid-century, when there was more social support for setting limits on adolescent behavior. In the 1990's, we parents are likely to have to take a stand on teenage freedoms that is not supported by the media or other institutions which have an impact on adolescent behavior.

One of the new freedoms available to adolescents is that of traveling alone, which can be an important introduction to new elements of our society. To be sure, many young children now travel alone to visit a divorced parent. But, such travel is usually closely supervised. Teenagers may travel for the same reason or other reasons, but are expected to be more independent and require less supervision. So, there are several principles of traveling we need to teach our teens, in order to help them avoid some of the pitfalls of traveling and have an enjoyable and rewarding experience. In a similar way, obtaining a driver's license provides opportunities for independent exploration of new facets of our society. And, again, there are some simple rules and limits we can set to help our teens balance the new freedoms and responsibilities involved in driving a car.

Another of the new responsibilities many teenagers take on is a job. Unfortunately, work today does not carry with it all of the positive attributes it once did. This is in part a result of the kind of work available to contemporary youth. In addition, research on working teenagers shows that those who work much more than fifteen hours per week are more likely to do poorly at school than those teenagers who work less than fifteen hours. Even so, more than 75 percent of teenagers now work at least some of the time, and they at least have an opportunity to learn some basic money management skills that will help them use their income wisely.

Of the new freedoms teenagers enjoy, one of the most troubling to parents is the listening to music and lyrics that may be sexually suggestive, violent, or demeaning of various groups. Adolescents often interpret this material differently than we do, so it is important for us to listen to this music ourselves, if we want to have credibility when we talk to our teens about it. We also need to keep in mind that some of the performers teenagers admire might seem to serve as role models for them, but this is usually not the case. Parents are still the primary role models for adolescents.

Other freedoms available to adolescents in our society are potentially more harmful. These include teenagers' access to alcohol, illegal drugs, and tobacco. Although young people have individual reasons for using and abusing these substances, this sort of behavior is also a result of the times in which we live. Due to increased availability and changing values, young people now face decisions about drug and alcohol use at earlier ages than they did at mid-century. This makes them more vulnerable, because they are less effective decision makers than they will be later in their lives. While there are a number of ways we parents can help teenagers make healthy choices in regard to alcohol, drugs, and tobacco, the most important step we can take is setting a good example of the responsible behavior we would like our teenagers to follow.

The extent of the stresses on contemporary teenagers is nowhere more evident than in the prevalence of adolescent suicide. We all need to be aware of the signs of emotional distress in young people, and be prepared to take immediate action if we observe these signs. A similar indication of the stresses on contemporary teenagers is the violence that is present not just in the larger society, but increasingly in our schools, as well. We need to attack this issue on a societal level, and also be ready to help individual teenagers who have been victims of or witnesses to violence.

Another of the sad lessons adolescents must learn about our society is that it is not always fair. This is often very painful, particularly the first time around. In addition to being supportive of teenagers at such times, we need to remind them of the many times when the society does operate fairly. This may be particularly difficult with homosexual teenagers, who tend to be discriminated against and socially ostracized. One indication of this is the disproportionate number of gay adolescents who commit suicide.

Unfairness and the balance between freedoms and responsibilities are also important issues in regard to the preservation of our environment, which has gained new importance since mid-century. Most of us now recognize our responsibility to do all that we can to protect our natural resources, including teaching our teenagers about environmental responsibility and setting a good example for them. In addition to focusing on environmental concerns, we also need to help teens appreciate the value of other forms of community service. We provide a lasting gift when we help adolescents discover the personal satisfaction that comes from participating in activities which benefit others, as well as oneself.

Our goals in helping our teenagers adapt to society are two-fold. One is to help these adolescents become independent and self-sufficient individuals. The other is to help them appreciate that we are all members of society and have responsibilities to our society, as well as to ourselves and our loved ones. To guide teenagers in both directions simultaneously, we need to show them how to make the distinctions needed to resolve this apparent contradiction. In this regard, as in others, our own example of independence combined with social responsibility is the best instruction we can provide.

TRAVELING SOLO

As a young man of 14, I traveled alone by train from Detroit to New York City. In those years just after World War II, child labor laws were not heavily enforced, and I was on my way to work as a busboy at my uncle's resort in the Catskills. When I arrived at Grand Central Station, I took a cab to the Dixie Hotel, where I was to catch a bus to the resort. The cabdriver asked me how much money I had, and I told him I had five dollars. When we finally reached the hotel, the fare — strangely enough — turned out to be precisely five dollars! Fortunately, I hadn't told the whole truth and had kept enough to buy my bus ticket. When I arrived at the resort and told my uncle of the long cab drive, he explained that the Dixie Hotel was only a few blocks from Grand Central and that I could have easily walked to it.

A lot has changed since those days, but many of the benefits and hazards for adolescents traveling alone remain the same. Traveling alone provides teenagers with a taste of independence, but it also puts them at risk in regard to those people who prey on naive travelers.

The Rewards and Risks of Going Alone

Traveling alone can teach adolescents a number of valuable lessons. First and foremost, of course, it teaches them about other people. When teenagers travel without the protection of parents who run interference for them, they experience the best and worst of dealing with strangers.

They encounter genuinely helpful and friendly people, as well as those who are thoughtless, aggressive, and dishonest.

Traveling alone also fosters a sense of autonomy and competence, a feeling that "I can cope — I can deal with the mysteries and unknowns of travel, and come out okay." But, most of all, traveling alone is exciting, romantic, and enjoyable for most adolescents, enabling them to see new places and hear new voices.

The newness of the experience, however, also makes lone young travelers attractive targets for those unscrupulous enough to take advantage of their inexperience. Teenagers have to be on their guard, not just against the opportunistic cabdrivers who overcharge, but also against thieves who are quick to snatch wallets, suitcases, or parcels left briefly unattended. In addition, teens may become the prey of hoodlums who are adept at using bullying and intimidation to take advantage of strangers in a strange land. Other hazards may involve sexual advances. One of my most frightening experiences as a teenager was being propositioned by a man in the men's room at Grand Central — needless to say, I got out of there very quickly!

What Parents Can Do

Preparing teenagers to travel alone is the single most important way we can help them. This entails discussing the situations and places to avoid, and reminding them often that strange places — for all the adventure they offer — can be very dangerous.

Preparation also includes reviewing the itinerary several times in advance, making sure everything the young person will need is packed, and ensuring that all the necessary money and documents are safely stored in an inside pocket or purse. We also should emphasize the need to be particularly alert and cautious when making transitions from one type of transportation to another. Transitions are where there is apt to be some confusion and the greatest chance of losing or forgetting things.

As for the human hazards, the rule taught to young children is one that can be followed by teenagers, as well: *don't talk to strangers.* Like all rules, however, this one has exceptions. There is usually no harm in a teenager's talking to someone in the next seat while on a train or airplane.

Once the hazards of a solo journey have been minimized by careful preparation, a teenager can fully realize the pleasures of traveling alone.

TAKING THE WHEEL

Obtaining a driver's license is an important milestone of maturity for contemporary teenagers. Much like a confirmation, a bar or bas mitzvah, a sweet-sixteen party, or a work permit, a driver's license signals that the adolescent has taken a major step toward adulthood. Such markers give young people a sense of direction — of where they have been, where they are now, and where they are going.

What Parents Can Do

Even before a teenager applies for a driver's license, you should discuss a number of practical considerations associated with driving. Perhaps the most important are finances. Teenagers need to be reminded that when we list them on our insurance policy as a driver of the family car, the insurance rates go up quite drastically. We also have to impress upon them that if they receive a ticket for a moving violation, this will further increase the cost of insurance.

If a teenager is going to use the car regularly, particularly to go to and from a job, we should ask for a contribution toward the car's upkeep and insurance. Even if the teen uses the car only on a limited basis, there should be an agreement about who is to pay for the gas, oil, car washes, and so on. (This sort of discussion is especially important if the teenager is given a hand-me-down car or purchases one of his or her own.)

We also need to set general guidelines for the use of the family car. This includes encouraging our teenagers to plan ahead for those times when they wish to use the car, and perhaps an occasional reminder that they cannot expect to have the car available at a moment's notice. We should also require teens to assume some family driving chores, such as chauffeuring their younger brothers and sisters, shopping, or picking up elderly relatives. On the other hand, we parents must be sensitive to our teens' needs, and we should try not to go back on a promise made as to when a teen can use the car.

Most teenagers *are* responsible drivers. Participation in SADD (Students Against Driving Drunk) both encourages responsibility and is an example of it. Nevertheless, a few kids do abuse their driving privileges. They may take too many other young people in the car, drive recklessly, or drink and drive. If a teenager abuses the right to drive, he or she should be grounded — quickly and firmly. How long a teen's driving privileges are suspended should depend on just how reckless he or she has been. Teenagers must learn that their freedom to drive is contingent upon their driving in a responsible manner.

On the other hand, it is important for us as parents not to over-react if a teenage driver who is usually careful receives a ticket or has a minor accident. More often than not, this is much more frightening to an adolescent than it is to us, and it teaches the teen to be more cautious in the future.

Driving a car is part of contemporary life, and teenagers who drive responsibly are accepting some of the conditions of being an adult. Although it may be sad for us to see them grow up so soon, it is also a relief to surrender the job of chauffeuring them.

TEENAGERS ON THE JOB

"If you want a car so badly, get a job, save up money, and buy yourself one." Most of us, I think, would applaud this father's response to his son's wish for a car. We have been brought up with the understanding that work has many benefits for adolescents. We believe that work teaches a teenager about the real world, about responsibility, about how to deal with people, and about the value of a dollar.

These assumptions about the value of work for adolescents have been challenged by a number of recent studies which explored the side effects of what they call *youthwork*. In their book, *When Teenagers Work*, Ellen Greenberger and Laurence Steinberg argue that youthwork no longer provides the benefits we used to believe it provided. According to Greenberger and Steinberg, "Experience in the adolescent workplace often breeds contempt for the idea that work can be enjoyable and satisfying. Extensive involvement in a job takes a toll on young people's education, and lower educational attainment has implications for young people's long-range occupational success and life satisfaction."

These authors go on to warn that intensive involvement in a job may lead to alcohol and drug abuse, especially when the job is stressful, and that the reward for working long hours — a fat paycheck — may not be so much of a good thing. It may lead teenagers, unencumbered by adult responsibilities, to engage in a level of consumption that is inconsistent with the obligations they will face in the coming years.

What Is the Value of Work?

To understand the changing value of work for adolescents, a little history may be helpful. Around the turn of the century, teenagers either worked or went to school. Teens who worked were already on the vocational track they would follow as adults. Those who did not work — usually the wealthier youth — were often on their way to college. Then, in the 1930's, the passage of child labor laws and compulsory education laws, as well as the provision of high school education for all youth, combined with the Depression to reduce considerably the number of young people who worked. It was only after mid-century, and the emergence of the fast food industry, that adolescents moved back into the work force in large numbers. Today, close to 75 percent of teenagers have some sort of a job.

The work teenagers engage in today — mainly in fast food restaurants — is different than the work teens engaged in before mid-century. Much of this new work is repetitious and often involves a lot of cleaning up. In addition, the irregular hours, lack of fringe benefits, and limited opportunities for advancement make youthwork discontinuous with adult work. Also, as indicated earlier, Greenberger and Steinberg report that when teenagers work long hours, their grades often drop. Even more disturbing is the researchers' finding that when educators know many young people in a school are working, they cut back on homework assignments.

Given these negative considerations, why do teenagers work? One reason is that there is now a youth culture with its own music, clothing styles, and language. To participate in this youth culture, teens need more money than parents may be willing or able to give them. From the adolescent's point of view, participating in the youth culture may be a necessity that makes work imperative. In addition, cars are virtually essential for many teenagers to get around, which adds pressure to earn money for transportation costs.

What Parents Can Do

One way to reduce the risks of youthwork is to insist that a teenager not work more than 15 hours a week. Studies show that teens who routinely work more than that are likely to pay the price in diminished school performance. We can also help adolescents learn some of the positive values of work by talking with them about their work experience. Even in fast food restaurants, young people may be learning much more than they think they are. If we encourage them to talk about the people they meet and work with, and about managerial styles, we help them discover how much they are learning about dealing with other people. At this time in history, when people skills are often as valuable as technical ones, this type of learning can be a very important benefit of youthwork.

MONEY MANAGEMENT FOR TEENS

During the summers of my adolescence, Sunday evenings were always times of great expectations. All week long, we busboys had waited on and catered to the guests who were about to check out of the resort hotel where I worked. Now, they had the opportunity to show their appreciation by giving us tips. The tips were, in fact, quite handsome, and for a teenager, I was earning a lot of money.

Making it was one thing. Managing it, however, was quite another. Being the youngest of six children, four of whom were boys, I had always worn the clothing my brothers had outgrown and so seldom had new things of my own. As soon as I had cash in hand, I was quick to go out and buy new clothes. This made me easy prey for salespeople who sensed my naivete and gullibility. I remember buying a suit that I knew I would never have any occasion to wear, but it was such a bargain — at least, so I was told — that I couldn't pass it up. After several purchases of this kind, I learned to spend my money more wisely.

I haul out these memories of another era because, in many ways, my experience is not unlike that of many contemporary teenagers, who are also able to earn money easily but may have trouble managing it. A recent survey suggests that only about 30 percent of employed high school seniors regularly put away money for their education or long-term savings. And, only 18 percent of employed high school students contribute some money toward family expenses. On the other hand, about 75 percent of employed high school seniors use some or all of their money for personal expenses — clothing, entertainment, recordings, and so on.

What Parents Can Do

As these spending patterns indicate, most teenagers do not help pay for their basic housing or living costs. Nor are they usually held responsible for their medical or dental expenses. One result is that teenagers today have the largest percentage of disposable income of any age group in our society. It is worthwhile, therefore, for teenagers to learn some simple rules of money management.

One of these rules is to *Save regularly.* Teenagers need to be encouraged to put away a small amount of their earnings on a regular basis. One way to encourage regular savings, if we can afford to do it, is to match the amount the teenager puts away with money of our own.

A second rule of money management is to *Budget.* We can help teenagers by sitting down with them and writing out what their income is, what their regular expenses are, and what they want to spend on clothing, recreation, eating out, and so on. Once teens have a good idea of what their net income actually is, they can set up realistic savings plans for large-ticket purchases. Working out a budget also helps a teenager prioritize potential purchases. And, if you happen to have a computer and a money management program, you and your teen can work together on developing an easy system for keeping track of income and expenses.

The third rule of money management is difficult to teach and to learn. The rule is, *Don't buy anything when you're under the sway of a strong emotion.* For some people, shopping can become a form of "therapy." While impulse buying can be useful and successful at times, talking the problem out is a much better idea and a lot cheaper.

In helping adolescents deal with money, we have to strike a delicate balance. While we want to help teenagers manage their money wisely, we also have to be careful not to intrude on their decision making. In the end, they must decide how they spend their money, no matter how foolish or irrational the decision may seem to us. Teens who earn money have also earned the freedom to choose how to spend it. Our responsibility as parents is to encourage teenagers to save, budget, and choose wisely, not to deprive them of their well-earned freedom of choice.

IT'S MUSIC TO THEIR EARS

Rock music is meaningful to teenagers for a variety of reasons. It is, first of all, a marker of a new level of mental maturity. Younger children are more visual and concerned with the here and now, whereas teenagers are more auditory and concerned with ideals and the future. Teenagers' infatuation with rock music is therefore evidence of their emergent ability to think in this new key. Rock music's appeal is also a marker of teens' new emotional maturity, reflecting their growing capacity to respond to the full range and depth of adult emotions which music can evoke.

Finally, music also serves as an identity marker for successive generations of young people. Just as each person must form an individual identity, each generation needs to find a group identity that is constructed not only of the political and social issues of the times, but also of the clothing, language, music, and performers of that particular era. When each successive generation reaches middle age, these same issues, clothing, language, music, and performers are usually resurrected as part of a nostalgia fad.

However, the involvement of teenagers with rock music — and now rap and rock videos — is not an unmixed blessing. As with so many other activities in life, something that is good in general can be made bad in particular. And, to use what may be an overly ripe metaphor, it only takes a few bad apples to give people the impression that a whole barrel of fruit has gone rotten. During the 1960's, for example, some rock groups did advocate drug use and contribute to the acceptance of drug use among teenagers. Today, a small number of rock groups, particularly those of the "heavy metal" variety, are so out of line with respect to obscene language and behavior that they reflect negatively on the whole rock music industry.

In her controversial book, *Raising PG Kids in an X-Rated Society*, Tipper Gore gives abundant and shocking examples of just how far these bad apples in the rock music barrel have gone. The language and actions of some of these heavy metal groups are particularly worrisome because these groups appeal to the youngest teenage groups — those least able to distance themselves from the performance. Unfortunately, these lurid lyrics and acts may be taken literally by the most vulnerable (and the least well-parented) teenagers. Some extreme rock groups apparently still fail to realize that liberty is not license, and freedom has to be balanced by a responsibility for the impact one's actions have on others, especially the young.

What Parents Can Do

Let us recognize first that the majority of rock groups — and their lyrics and videos — are not really harmful to adolescents, and that this music does in fact serve some important functions for teenagers.

Given this recognition, what can we do about the bad apples? I agree with Tipper Gore that the solution is not censorship, but rather enhanced awareness combined with parental and community involvement. The printing of lyrics on the jackets of recordings is one positive result of Tipper Gore's book and the efforts of her group, The Parents' Music Resource Center. Now, at least, we can check in advance on the lyrics of songs our teenager might wish to buy.

However busy we may be, we need to take the time to check out lyrics and videos our teens are interested in, and occasionally accompany them (particularly the younger ones) to concerts. If we make the effort to become familiar with the lyrics our teenagers are listening to — and to watch what they are watching — we have credibility when we express our opinion regarding the value of the music.

One of the most important skills we can teach our teenagers is the ability to discriminate between what is exploitative and what is artistic and worthwhile. We can also take comfort in the knowledge that, in the end, it is the higher quality music and performers that will become part of our teenagers' group identity. It is to this music and these performers that they will return when, at middle age, it is their generation's turn to be nostalgic.

TEENAGE IDOLS

I recently asked a group of young people to watch a video-tape of interviews with some "heavy metal" rock stars, as well as clips from some of their live concerts and music videos. The tape, put out by the Parents' Music Resource Center — an Arlington, Virginia group that monitors popular music and music videos — presented a picture of young men who were deliberately crude and obscene, enthusiastic about drug and alcohol abuse, sexually violent, and disdainful of women. I wanted students to tell me what made these musicians popular among — and possible role models for — young adolescents.

The students, however, did not respond to either the material or the performers with the revulsion I had felt. Even the feminists in the class were more amused than shocked. Most of the students said that they had never thought about the values conveyed by the music. And, more often than not, they said they did not even listen to the lyrics. When they did listen, they thought of the words as a joke or as satirical, rather than as an expression of the singer's true feelings and attitudes. In any case, they did not see these musicians as role models either for themselves or for younger adolescents. And, when we talked about other, more socially responsible musicians, the students did not see them as role models either.

The reactions of these students reinforced the results of a number of studies dealing with the adults young people admire and model themselves after. These studies indicate that while younger teenagers often develop strong emotional ties to pop idols, this is more a sign of their newly discovered status as teenagers than of any serious identification with, say, Guns N' Roses or 2 Live Crew. A recent Gallup poll of young people supports this viewpoint. When asked to name the person they most admired, the majority chose a parent or some other relative.

Although most adolescents see the extreme rock and rap groups as merely a parody of adults' erroneous image of "wild youth," some do not. In my experience, teenagers who identify with such anarchistic performers — and who adopt their values and attitudes — are already troubled and adrift. These teens are often the victims of neglect, abandonment, and abuse. They readily identify with the anger and rebellion toward adult society that is expressed by these groups, whose music allows them to vent their resentment of a society that has left them unguided, uncared for, and unprotected.

Fortunately, most adolescents neither identify with nor imitate the anti-social language, attitudes, and behavior of these musical groups. Most teens say that such groups actually paint a picture of young people that is neither accurate nor fair. "That's not how we look or act," say teenagers. "But, it's how our parents *think* we look and act." While these rock groups are not a menace to the manners and morals of such teens, they do highlight some misperceptions between the generations.

What Parents Can Do

Forewarned is forearmed. Once we realize that teenagers think we see them as they are portrayed by some music groups, we can disabuse them of this notion by telling them that we do not see young people as wild or awful. This will enhance our already privileged position as parents, and help us continue to be our children's most significant role models.

It sometimes happens, however, that an adolescent will take a rock star as a role model and imitate him or her to an uncomfortable extent. Teenagers who do this usually feel inadequate and seek to identify with a popular rock star as a way of vicariously attaining a sense of positive self-regard. Rather than challenge the teen's dress or behavior, we need to do all that we honestly can to praise the teen's personal talents and abilities, and make him or her feel more adequate. Sometimes, it helps to say something like, "You know, you really are good and decent, and I not only love you as a parent, I really like you as a person." Saying this sort of thing many times and in many different ways is probably the best way to help a teenager grow out of over-identifying with a rock star.

TEENAGE ABUSE
OF ILLEGAL DRUGS

The availability of illegal drugs remains a serious threat to adolescents in the 1990's, decades after drug abuse among teenagers took a very marked upswing during the 1960's and 1970's. Fortunately, however, most recent surveys suggest that the use of illegal drugs by teenagers is leveling off or even declining a bit. Use of marijuana, hashish, stimulants, and sedatives is continuing to decline. And, another encouraging sign is a decrease in the use of cocaine by high school seniors. After a rapid rise between 1983 and 1986, the use of crack — a dangerous form of smokable cocaine — seems to have leveled off and may be declining.

Nonetheless, about 1 in every 6 or 7 high school seniors has tried cocaine, and 1 in 18 has tried crack. In addition, while the percentage of teenagers using illegal drugs may not be growing, the age at which teens experiment with drugs appears to be decreasing. In general, there appears to be a sharp increase in illegal drug use between the sixth and seventh grade, when many young adolescents move into junior high school.

Why Teenagers Use Drugs

Young people from all backgrounds abuse illegal drugs. However, the highest rates of abuse by minors are found in impoverished and segregated communities, such as ghettos, barrios, and reservations. In these settings, there is a combination of *social* risk factors — including high unemployment, poverty, poor school facilities, social isolation, criminal role models, and gang influence — which are all associated with the use of illegal drugs.

In addition to the social risk factors listed above, there are a number of *personal* risk factors that can also dispose young people to use illicit drugs. One of the most powerful personal risk factors in adolescent drug use is parental example. Young people whose parents use illegal drugs are much more likely to do the same than teenagers whose parents do not use such drugs. Other personal risk factors associated with teenage drug abuse include a lack of religious affiliation, a great deal of family conflict, anti-social and anti-authority attitudes, and lack of achievement motivation. The greater the number of these personal risk factors in a teenager's life, the more likely he or she is to turn to drugs.

Once a teen starts to use drugs to deal with unhappiness, depression, and day-to-day pressures, the usage often becomes habitual and is carried into young adulthood. The consequences can be serious and long lasting. A recent study examined 1,000 high school students who began using a certain drug in high school and were continuing to use it as young adults. Those who used marijuana or other illegal drugs were in poorer physical health, had more dysfunctional job and marital histories, and were more likely to have been delinquent than were non-users.

What Parents Can Do

Although there are now many drug education and drug use prevention programs in operation throughout the country, they will not be sufficient to solve the problem. The unfortunate reality is that knowledge of the harm done by drugs does not outweigh the pressure to use drugs generated by any combination of the risk factors described above. The only sure way to reduce drug use among teenagers is to reduce the number and extent of the risk factors that lead them to seek escape from stress through drugs.

We live in a complex and difficult society, where it is often impossible to lessen or eliminate all the pressures that lead adolescents to take the risk of using illegal drugs. But, the fact that we can't do everything does not mean that we can do nothing. If we appreciate that conflict in the home can add to the pressures a teenager experiences, we can try to reduce such conflict by negotiation, rather than continuing to engage in fights and arguments. We can examine our teen's schedule and make sure that he or she is not overburdened with school and extracurricular activities. Perhaps most importantly, we can say and mean that we will be there to listen whenever our teenager wants or needs to talk.

By taking these steps and doing whatever else we can to remove or reduce the pressures and risk factors in adolescents' lives, we are fulfilling our responsibilities as parents and concerned citizens. But, if our teenager does begin to use illegal drugs, professional intervention is warranted. The toll-free help line listed at the end of the next section can be a source of information about counseling and treatment.

TEENS AND ALCOHOL

Alcohol abuse is widespread among today's teenagers. According to the National Council on Alcoholism and Drug Dependence, the average age at which young people in our society begin to drink alcoholic beverages is 12. About 4 percent of our high school seniors use alcohol daily, while 92 percent have tried it. And, millions of teens have had adverse experiences caused by excessive drinking. One result of all this youthful alcohol consumption is that alcohol-related motor-vehicle accidents are the leading cause of death for Americans between 15 and 24 years old.

Children's first encounter with alcohol use is usually the example set by adults at home (a parent seen drinking a beer while watching television, or a sipping a cocktail before dinner). In addition, a child will see alcohol consumed an average of 75,000 times on television before he or she reaches the drinking age. But, the immediate pressure to use alcohol comes from peers, and this pressure starts early. In a national survey, 25 percent of fourth graders said they felt "some" to "a lot" of peer pressure to try beer, wine, or liquor. By the time the children reach seventh grade, about 60 percent said they felt this pressure to try alcohol. The motivations for using alcohol were primarily "to feel older" and "to have a good time."

The widespread abuse of alcohol by teenagers puts a large number of them at risk for addiction. According to the Alcohol, Drug Abuse, and Mental Health Administration, it may take an adult up to 10 years to become addicted, but a teenager can become addicted to alcohol in 6 months or less. The reason is when teenagers begin to drink, they do so in such quantities that the addiction process sets in more quickly. In addition, their body chemistry hastens the addiction process. As a result, there are now more than 2 million alcoholic teenagers in America.

Problem drinking among teenagers usually develops in four stages. During the first — *experimental* — stage, an adolescent tries out alcohol and likes its effect. At the next stage, the teen begins to *seek out opportunities* to drink, and there are noticeable behavioral changes. He or she may choose new friends, become less concerned about personal appearance or schoolwork, and show moderate weight gain or loss as well as unusual irritability or passivity. Alcohol *dependency* becomes evident at the third stage, when an alcohol-induced high becomes the young person's top priority. At this point, the teen is likely to steal, skip school, and show marked changes in eating and sleeping habits. At the fourth — *addicted* — stage, the teen needs alcohol to feel normal. And, at this critical stage, all of the other symptoms intensify.

What Parents Can Do

Parents who do not abuse drugs or alcohol themselves provide teenagers with the best armor against substance abuse. In addition, when we do everything we can to give teens a supportive home base and a good sense of self-esteem, when we listen without judging them, and when we give them a sense of our own values and standards, we provide them with the inner strength to deal with life's stressors.

With this inner strength, they need not look to alcohol to help them solve their problems.

If, however, we do suspect that our teenager is abusing alcohol, it is important not to deny the fact. Although alcohol abuse *is* painful to deal with, the earlier we confront the problem, the better for everyone. If we fail to take action, it appears that we either condone this behavior or don't care enough to do anything about it. Clearly, neither message is a healthy one for parents to send to a teenager with a drinking problem.

If a teen's drinking is becoming a problem, it is important for parents to set firm rules about drinking, and to state in advance the consequences of breaking those rules. If the problem is more serious and the teenager is addicted, a parent should seek — and help the teenager understand the need for — professional counselling and treatment.

The nationwide toll-free help line, 1-800-554-KIDS, is open from 9 to 5 EST, Monday through Friday. It can give you information and refer you to local sources of help if your child is having trouble with alcohol or other drugs.

TEENS AND TOBACCO

I began smoking when I was 14 and working as a busboy at my uncle's resort during the summers. The waitresses I worked with smoked and did not discourage me from starting. This was in the 1950's, when there was little talk about the dangers of smoking, and cigarette packs did not carry warning labels. Smoking seemed like a grown-up and sophisticated thing to do.

My experience, it turns out, was fairly typical. According to the American Lung Association, young people who smoke cigarettes daily often develop the habit between the ages of 11 and 14. Even today, when the dangers of smoking are well-publicized, many young people begin to smoke for the same reason I did — because family members, friends, or co-workers smoke.

Peers play an especially important role in a teenager's decision to smoke. Teens are interested in doing whatever they perceive everyone else to be doing, even something as unhealthy as smoking cigarettes. The good news, however, is that the percentage of high school seniors who smoke cigarettes daily decreased from 29 percent in 1976 to about 19 percent in 1991.

Of course, the best way for a young person not to develop the habit is never to start in the first place. And, educational campaigns against smoking are changing the way that young people think about smokers. In one study, 76 percent of all high school seniors said that they would face peer disapproval if they smoked a pack of cigarettes daily. In some states, raising the price of cigarettes has also contributed to a decline in the numbers of teenagers who smoke.

Encouraging an individual teenager who already smokes to stop, however, is another story. A teen may stop once she discovers a strong motivator, such as realizing that cigarettes leave her too short of breath to play well on the school basketball team. Or, she may stop if she becomes friendly with a group that looks down on people who smoke.

What Parents Can Do

For parents, discovering that a teenager has started smoking is extremely distressing. It is difficult to watch a child — whom we have tried to protect from danger all her life — expose herself to something that has been proven to be deadly. Unfortunately, we cannot simply force a teen to stop smoking. Moreover, our teen is likely to feel that she is not vulnerable to the serious illnesses linked to smoking, such as cancer. Hence, she will often dismiss our warnings about the dangers of cigarettes as having no relevance for her.

If warnings don't help, what does? Research shows that children are more likely to smoke if their parents smoke. Conversely, when parents stop smoking, their children usually follow their example — by either not taking up the habit or giving it up if they have already begun. For this reason, giving up cigarettes is a vital means of encouraging our teenagers not to smoke.

As for those of us parents who are non-smokers, we need
to make it clear that while we may not be able to prevent our
teen from smoking, we will not tolerate smoking anywhere
in the house. We can also help our teen find a personal
motivation — such as the fact that smoking turns your teeth
yellow and makes your breath smell bad — for giving up
cigarettes. This can be a pivotal step in helping a teenager
decide to kick the cigarette habit.

TEENAGE SUICIDE

"If only I can get back to Majorca," my teenage psychiatric patient said, "everything will be all right." This young man had spent a long, joyous winter holiday on the Spanish island of Majorca — a much needed reprieve from a tumultuous and destructive family environment. It was the happiest period in his life, and he believed that he would be magically reborn into a more loving and accepting family if he could only return there. Some months after he was discharged from the private psychiatric hospital where I had treated him, I read that he had put an end to his life.

Twenty-five years ago, when this incident occurred, teenage suicide was relatively rare. Unhappily, the teenage suicide rate has tripled since mid-century, and there has been a comparable increase in the number of teens who attempt suicide or have suicidal thoughts. A recent survey of 1,986 teens listed in *Who's Who Among American High School Students* found that 30 percent of these young people had considered suicide, 4 percent had attempted it, and 60 percent said they knew a peer who had attempted or committed suicide. It is estimated that more than 5,000 teens take their own life each year.

The Dynamics of Suicide

Teenagers commit or attempt to commit suicide for many different reasons. The *precipitating* cause is usually some traumatic experience, such as losing a parent, breaking up with a boyfriend or girlfriend, not getting into a coveted college, or losing an important competition. Such an event activates long-standing *predisposing* causes, such as abiding feelings of inadequacy, inferiority, persecution, or injustice. The adolescent feels that there is no way out — no way for things to get better — and cannot bear the thought of continued emotional pain.

The increase in the teenage suicide rate over the past few decades may reflect the increase in the stressors experienced by adolescents. Today's teens face problems different than those faced by teens of previous generations. For example, they have more freedom and opportunity to become sexually active and to abuse drugs. They experience more loss (of a parent and of security) due to the drastic increase in the divorce rate. And, on another level, many young people have also lost their belief in progress — the sense that the world is becoming a better place in which to live, work, and raise a family.

Teenagers are often reluctant to reveal their thoughts or discuss the problems they are experiencing. Unfortunately, many teens also conceal their pains and fears, so that even their parents and closest friends have no idea that they are suffering and considering suicide.

Nonetheless, while many adolescents give no indication of an impending suicide attempt, others do. A telling symptom is a dramatic change in the young person's mood and dealings with other people. Continual anger and irritability, frequent complaints of boredom, and increased risk taking can all be indications of depression and accompanying suicidal thoughts.

What Parents Can Do

Any intimation that a teenager is contemplating suicide should be taken seriously. The young person is in crisis, and what he or she needs most is a sympathetic parent who is willing to listen and not to judge. What may seem superficial to us, such as losing a ball game, may have taken on enormous emotional significance for the teenager. It is very important not to dismiss or undervalue these feelings.

In talking with a teenager whom we suspect has suicidal ideas, it is best to be frank and ask the teen directly whether he or she has thought of suicide. It is often a relief for an adolescent to admit having such ideas. We should also arrange for the teenager to meet with a mental health professional schooled in suicide prevention. Suicide-prevention centers are available in most communities, as are suicide hot lines, which can be found in the phone book under "Suicide."

WHEN VIOLENCE STRIKES

It was a street fight — two young men beating up a third. Passers-by, including myself, shouted at them to stop; others summoned the police, who arrived quickly and subdued the attackers. I rushed over to the victim. He was shaking and blood was running from his nose, which he was wiping off with his fist. He was trying hard to control himself, but there were tears in his eyes. I handed him my handkerchief, and we talked for a bit. "Bastards," he cursed, gradually regaining his composure.

Unfortunately, teenagers today are more likely than ever to see or experience violence. When a person is victimized or is a witness to violent actions (in real life — not on television, where there is no immediate danger), he or she reacts with a sequence of "fight or flight" responses: adrenaline is pumped into the bloodstream, the heart rate increases, and breathing becomes more rapid. Once the danger has passed, vital signs return to normal and the person begins to think about the experience. In the incident described above, it was only after the young man had calmed down that he was able to curse his attackers.

Traumatic events are burned into our memories and continue to exert their influence long after the physical reactions have subsided. It is not uncommon for a victim or witness to have bouts of uncontrollable sobbing or shaking some time after a violent encounter. Often, the stressful event is also re-lived in dreams and night terrors. In addition, a person may develop phobias (inappropriate fears) of places similar to the locale where the attack took place, or of people who resemble the attackers.

Other possible long-term effects of being a victim or witness include anxiety attacks, an inability to concentrate, aimlessness, and chronic depression. And, no matter how secure and self-assured a teenager may seem, no one is immune to such reactions.

How Parents Can Help

A teenager who has suffered a violent experience needs immediate comfort, support, and reassurance that the danger has passed. In addition to medical attention, an adolescent who has been victimized might well benefit from professional help in dealing with the psychological effects. Such help is particularly important if the teenager shows no emotion or insists he is "okay," but exhibits behavioral or physical clues that all is not well. When teenagers attempt to deny the experience of violence, they put themselves at risk for post-traumatic stress syndrome — in other words, manifesting any or all of the previously described stress symptoms at a later time.

If one of our teenagers becomes a victim of violence or a witness to it, our concern for the teen is compounded by our own anger at the perpetrator. While such feelings are natural, we should not let them consume us. Our first responsibility is to give the teen emotional support and, if necessary, professional help. We also need to provide reassurance that he or she did not invite or incite the incident.

As parents, we cannot root out all the world's injustices, but we can help our children cope effectively with one of the unfortunate aspects of the human condition.

UNFAIR! UNFAIR!

"We didn't do anything wrong, but we're being punished," a group of high school students told me recently during a visit to their school. "It's so unfair."

A few days earlier, a janitor had found marijuana butts in one of the boys' bathrooms. In response, the principal had locked *all* of the restrooms on the same side of the building, declaring that they would stay locked until the young men responsible came forward. It was a large building, and closing the bathrooms meant that many teens had to walk a long distance to the other bathrooms, which were overcrowded and messy from excessive use.

When I talked with the principal, he said that he really had no other choice: unless he took tough measures, the kids would continue to smoke pot in school. I told him that many of the students felt that they were being unfairly punished, and he admitted that he hoped peer pressure would prompt the guilty young men to confess. (I learned later that it did not, and that a group of concerned parents forced the principal to re-open the bathrooms.)

Unfairness is a common experience for adolescents, and it can come in many forms. For example, one girl might be chosen for the lead in the school play not because she is best suited for the role, but because her parents are friendly with the school's music director. To many teenagers who are extremely self-conscious, it might seem that nature itself is unfair. Every teen can tell you about the "perfect" classmate who seems to have it all: good looks, intelligence, athletic ability, *and* popularity.

What Parents Can Do

There are several ways in which teenagers and their parents can respond to instances of unfairness. In the case of the strict principal, for example (who, despite his good intentions, was wrong to punish the entire student body), parents took action and the unfairness was stopped.

There may be times, however, when neither teenagers nor their parents have any recourse but to accept the situation. While logic tells us that unfairness is part of life, when it happens to a teenager we love, remaining logical may prove difficult for us and our teen.

Encouraging and supporting our adolescents in expressing their anger and resentment should be our first order of business. Let your teenager know that it is okay to feel angry and that he or she should let off some steam, even if it means going into the bathroom and screaming, or finding some other outlet for frustration.

Once the teen has calmed down, you can talk about some of your own experiences with unfairness. If you tell about the time your entire tenth-grade class received a week's detention because one student played a practical joke on the teacher, you help an adolescent see that everyone — including parents — has had to deal with unfair treatment at some point.

In addition, we can remind our teenagers that growing angry at unfair treatment is fine, but they also need to savor those times when things do go right and justice is served. Adolescents should understand that life can indeed be unfair, but such times are definitely the exception, not the rule.

ATTITUDES TOWARD HOMOSEXUALITY

It must have been a powerful experience, because I can still remember it now, some four decades later. When I was in junior high school, I was endlessly preoccupied with well-endowed girls. But, one day, while waiting in the lunch line, I noticed the buttocks of a young man in front of me and had an impulse to touch them. The impulse shocked me, and I became very anxious — afraid I was homosexual. Eventually, I accepted the fact that the impulse was a one-time occurrence and my sexual inclinations were overwhelmingly toward girls.

After I became a psychologist and had studied such matters, I discovered that for adolescents, a passing attraction to a member of the same sex is the norm, not the exception. A review of available research found that certain types of sex play occur fairly frequently in groups of boys between the ages of 8 and 13. And, about 10 percent of boys and 5 percent of girls may engage in sexual relations with a member of the same sex at least once during adolescence.

Fleeting same-sex attractions occur primarily because young adolescents are experiencing strong sexual urges at an age when they are still intimidated by members of the opposite sex. Unconsciously, it is more comfortable to direct these feelings toward a member of the same sex. Unless this attraction is accompanied by persistent erotic dreams and fantasies about a person of the same sex, however, it is probably not an indication of an abiding homosexual orientation.

While an early adolescent same-sex attraction is common, it can also be — as it was for me — anxiety arousing. This anxiety is partly a result of the many myths and prejudices regarding homosexuality. The current controversies over homosexual individuals in the military and discussing homosexual lifestyles in the classroom are evidence that these myths and prejudices remain widespread.

What Parents Can Do

I once asked my three teenage sons what they knew about homosexuality. They giggled, and one said homosexuals talked and walked funny. I acknowledged that although some homosexuals do talk or walk "funny," the majority do not. "Most homosexuals," I said, "look and behave like anyone else, and they are found in all cultures and all of the professions." I also told them that we all go through a period in early adolescence when we have sexual feelings for the same sex. I then talked about my own teenage experience and said, "It could happen to you. If anything, it means you are normal." They winced and put on their give-me-a-break expressions.

As we separated, one of my sons quietly said in a relieved tone, "Thanks, Dad." The effort it took to have that talk was more than repaid by his thanks.

Some parents have to confront a more troubling situation — when their teenager confides that he or she is homosexual. Accepting a teenager's homosexuality is not easy, but parents can take comfort that their child felt secure enough about their love to talk with them about this difficult issue. And, parents should rest assured that their child's homosexuality does not reflect on the job they've done as parents. If they also reassure their teenager that he or she is still loved and will be treated the same as ever, they can help the entire family avoid unnecessary conflict and pain.

A CONCERN FOR THE ENVIRONMENT

Some years ago, when I taught at the University of Rochester, there was widespread concern about the pollution of Lake Ontario, so a "Walk for Water" was organized. Teenagers enlisted sponsors to pay (a quarter in this case) for every mile they walked. The money they earned went toward water testing and pollution-control activities. On the day of the walk, I drove past thousands of cheerful young people walking in an orderly fashion for many miles in their efforts to combat pollution, and I thought to myself, "I really have underestimated these teenagers; they truly are much more committed and unselfish than I had supposed."

The next day, I drove along the same route I had taken the day before, but this time I saw a number of sanitation crews busily cleaning up all the debris the teenagers had left on their "Walk for Water." My immediate reaction was to think, "What hypocrites! These teenagers were walking to clean up the environment, but they probably cost the city more money to clean up their mess than they earned by walking!"

I soon realized, however, that there was a developmental rather than a "hypocritical" explanation for the behavior I had witnessed. Thanks to the new mental abilities they acquire around the age of 12 or 13, most teenagers become capable of imagining an ideal world. Nevertheless, they are still too inexperienced to appreciate the many barriers to overcome — and the amount of time and effort required — to realize even a small portion of their ideals. On the contrary, many teenagers believe that if you can imagine a world without war, avarice, or pollution, then it should be possible to create such a world almost immediately.

Another reason teens might not fully grasp the complexity of environmental issues is that they may not yet possess the highly abstract knowledge needed to understand such issues. To fully appreciate the problem of water pollution, for example, requires an understanding of chemistry and biology, as well as the economic considerations that underlie acid rain.

In other respects, teenagers are really no different than adults. Some of us are simply apathetic, but even those of us who are concerned often have difficulty finding the time and energy to do the intellectual work needed to grasp an environmental problem fully — much less take effective action regarding it — unless we are immediately affected by it. Still, we probably should make time to help our teenagers increase their understanding of environmental issues.

What Parents Can Do

In general, a true concern for preserving the environment grows from an appreciation of nature's beauties and bounties, as well as its catastrophes. We can begin to instill this appreciation in young people by enjoying nature with them and giving them responsibility for the care of plants and animals. We can also enlist their help in sorting the family's newspapers, cans, and bottles for recycling. And, we can teach them to create and use compost in order to reuse food scraps and enrich our gardens. If we are so inclined, we might even have them join us in collecting signatures on a petition regarding local environmental issues.

In the end, it is our appreciation of nature — and our own efforts, both big and small, to preserve it — that will have the most lasting and beneficial impact on our teenagers and our planet.

HABITS OF THE HEART

"Habits of the heart" is a phrase Alexis de Tocqueville used more than 150 years ago to describe the value Americans placed on helping one another. Today, this remains an ongoing and powerful value for many members of our society. We see these "habits of the heart" in the spontaneous outpouring of gifts for the needy when there has been a natural catastrophe. We also see it, for example, in the efforts of college students to find shelter for the street people of Boston when the temperature drops below freezing. Activities such as these are so commonplace that we tend to take them for granted, overlooking the extraordinary willingness of people in our society to extend themselves for others in need.

A Decline in Altruism?

Parents generally recognize the value of community service in building a young person's character. However, we tend to emphasize this more for children than for adolescents, and there is evidence that young people today may be less endowed with "habits of the heart" than earlier generations. A survey by Yankelovich, Clancy, Schulman found that young people between the ages of 18 and 34 do not place community service high among their values.

While the commitment of contemporary youth to "habits of the heart" may be less than it has been in the recent past, there is also evidence that such commitment has waxed and waned over the entire course of our nation's history. We may, therefore, have only encountered a temporary down-swing. And, the large number of teenagers who now work in addition to going to school face real limits on their ability to volunteer for social projects.

Many organizations continue to do their part to keep "habits of the heart" alive and well. Groups ranging from Boys Clubs to Girl Scouts, Camp Fire to Red Cross, and 4-H to YMCA foster the spirit of citizenship and community service today among millions of young people from all races, religions, ethnic backgrounds, and socio-economic levels.

Schools have recognized the value of community service, as well. Hundreds of public high schools offer community service courses, although mostly as electives. And, some communities have recognized the importance of public service by making it a full-credit course required for graduation.

What Parents Can Do

When one of my sons was in high school, he participated in a community service program that involved him in visiting the elderly in a nursing home on a regular basis. I wondered, given all the other things he was doing, whether this wasn't a bit much to take on. But, he enjoyed it and felt very good about making a contribution of some sort. Since then, he has maintained an interest in various community projects and wants to pursue a career in environmental protection.

I cite this example because I believe that my own luke-warm attitude toward community service was not unusual. Perhaps, it is the attitude of *our* generation (soured as we were on government service after the Vietnam War and Watergate) that is responsible for the decline of interest in public service among contemporary adolescents. Looking back, I know that if I had it to do over again, I would be much more supportive of my son's involvement in volunteer service projects.

We are beginning to recognize, I think, that many of our problems as a society — including our economic problems — derive from an exaggerated individualism and self-centeredness. In order to solve these problems, we need to restore our sense of community, and re-discover the truth that inter-dependence is as healthy and important as independence. By instilling and supporting community spirit in our teenagers, we do something very beneficial for them, for our society, and most certainly for ourselves. In so doing, we can all re-learn the "habits of the heart."

AFTERWORD

You have now had a chance to consider and possibly put into practice some of the information and advice offered in this book. I hope that the book has helped you to appreciate the many issues — large and small — that teenagers are confronting at home, at school, and in the larger community.

Adolescents are complex, and part of their complexity lies in the fact that they are making the transition from childhood to adulthood. In part, however, their complexity also derives from the rapidly changing world in which they have to find their way to an independent, responsible adulthood.

If what you have read has given you insights into your teenager's behavior, and helped you deal with one or more difficult situations, then the book has achieved what I hoped it would. I must confess, however, that if the book has succeeded in this way, I cannot really take the credit. Instead, I have to thank all the parents and teenagers with whom I have worked over the years, and from whom I learned so much.

What they have taught me, and what I have tried to convey in these chapters, is that despite a rapidly changing and increasingly stressful world, and despite the adolescent storms and stress and parental mid-life struggles, it is still possible for adolescents and their parents to show one another love, kindness, thoughtfulness, and respect. And, it is because I have learned this lesson that I look to the future world — which today's adolescents will inhabit — with cautious optimism.

INDEX

BIBLIOGRAPHY

Brandino, J., Brann, S., Coatsworth, S., Sonzensa, H., Swain, C., & Tulao, F. *Raising Each Other: A Book for Teens and Parents*. Alameda, CA: Hunter House, 1988.

Brenner, Barbara. *A Killing Season*. New York, NY: Four Winds Press/Macmillan Child Group, 1984.

Coleman, James S., & Hoffer, Thomas. *Public and Private High Schools: The Impact of Communities*. New York, NY: Basic Books.

Elkind, David. *All Grown Up and No Place to Go: Teenagers in Crisis*. Reading, MA: Addison Wesley, 1984.

Faber, Adele., & Mazlish, Elaine. *How to Talk So Kids Will Listen and Listen So Kids Will Talk*. New York, NY: Avon Books, 1989.

Frank, Anne. *The Diary of a Young Girl*. New York, NY: Modern Library, Random House, 1978.

Ginott, H. *Between Parent and Teenager*. New York, NY: Avon, 1960.

Gore, Tipper. *Raising PG Kids in an X-Rated Society*. Nashville, TN: Abingdon Press, 1987.

Herbert, Frank. The Dune Series. New York, NY: Ace Books (Division of Berkley Books), 1986 - 1987.

L'Engle, Madeleine. *A Swiftly Tilting Planet*. New York, NY: Dell Books, 1981.

L'Engle, Madeleine. *A Wind In The Door*. New York, NY: Dell Books, 1976.

Lindberg, Charles A. *The Spirit of St Louis*. Cutchogue, NY: Buccaneer Books, 1991.

Norman, Jane. & Harris, Myron W. *The Private Life of the American Teenager*. New York, NY: Rawson-Wade.

Pascal, Francine. *Sweet Valley High*. New York, NY: Bantam, 1989.

Pederson, A. & O'Mara, P. (Ed.s). *Teens: A Fresh Look*. Santa Fe, NM: John Muir Publications, 1991.

Schwarz, M., (ed.). *TV and Teens*. Reading, MA: Addison-Wesley, 1982.

Staley, B. *Between Form and Freedom: A Practical Guide to the Teen Years*. Wallbridge, England: Hawthorne, 1988.

Strasburger, V. *Getting Your Kids to Say No in the 90's*. New York, NY: Simon & Schuster, 1993.

Toth, Susan Allen. *Blooming: A Small Town Girlhood*. New York, NY: Little, Brown & Co., 1992.

Viorst, Judith. *Necessary Losses*. New York, NY: Fawcett Crest, 1987.

Wallerstein, Judith. *Second Chances: Men, Women & Children a Decade After Divorce*. New York, NY: Ticknor & Fields, 1989.

Winship, E.C. *Reaching Your Teenager*. New York, NY: Houghton-Miflin, 1983.